To the caring, hard-working and skilled Supported Education Coordinators we have the privilege to know and work with in the state of Washington. We admire and respect your unwavering commitment to the ideals of recovery through work with your students, fellow coordinators and the many sectors of the mental health, education and wider communities in which you thrive.

SUPPORTED EDUCATION FOR PEOPLE WITH PSYCHIATRIC DISABILITIES

A Practical Manual

Jolyn Wells-Moran
Deanne Gilmur

University Press of America,® Inc.
Lanham · New York · Oxford

4720 Boston Way
Lanham, Maryland 20706
UPA Acquisitions Department (301) 459-3366

12 Hid's Copse Rd.
Cumnor Hill, Oxford OX2 9JJ

Printed in the United States of America
British Library Cataloging in Publication Information Available

ISBN: 978-0-7618-2348-3

CONTENTS

FIGURES

ACKNOWLEDGEMENTS

We wish to thank the State of Washington Department of Social and Health Services, Mental Health Division, for their valuable part in supporting the creation of this manual.

We also gratefully thank Lynne Braedt, Kathy Harris, Sunshine Allen, Wayne C.R. Taylor, Susan Peabody and Tom Moran for all of the excellent, sensitive and grammatically correct editing and format recommendations. Without their help, this book would have been far less user-friendly

INTRODUCTION

This Manual

Supported Education (SEd) Programs can differ in design and setting, but every program needs a mission, a program description, job descriptions, and policies and procedures to guide it. The authors, called the Partnership for the Development of Supported Education, developed these materials and more for a generic manual that could be individualized by Washington State programs they assist in development.

The Partners are Deanne Gilmur, M.Ed., who directs Patient and Family Education, Pierce College at Western State Hospital, of which Pierce SEd is a part, and Jolyn Wells-Moran, Ph.D., M.S.W., Executive Director, Center for Psychiatric Recovery and Rehabilitation Education (CPRRE), who has also directed the Consumer-To-Provider Training Program (CTP), now part of CPRRE, for the past nine years.

The Partnership emerged from the placement of a CTP student, Lynn Braedt, in an internship in 1996 with the newly forming SEd Program at the Pierce College space on the campus of Western State Hospital in Lakewood, near Tacoma, Washington. The program would serve consumers of mental health services in the Pierce Regional Support Network. Huss Malik, Ph.D., then managing the CTP contract at the Mental Health Division (MHD), Washington State DSHS, and simultaneously managing a contract for the initial development of the Pierce SEd Program suggested the Pierce SEd Program as a possible field placement. This was the second SEd Program in the state. The first was operated by PACE on the eastern side of the state in Spokane, called SEER, through the Institute for Extended Learning and located at Spokane Falls Community College.

To understand parts of this Manual, readers should know that the Consumer-To-Provider Training Program trains for, and places people with psychiatric disabilities into, mental health employment. Begun in 1993, the CTP Training Program is based on the Regional Assessment and Training Center (RATC) model in Denver, Colorado, which has been training and placing consumer-providers, or prosumers, for over fifteen years.

The success of Braedt in her field placement role at Pierce SEd, then later as its Program Coordinator, prompted Gilmur to propose that other SEd programs be initiated and developed in the same way. Training students in the Consumer-To-Provider (CTP) Training Program so they develop certain helping skills necessary to working with other people who have psychiatric disabilities would be the first step. Then, students would be trained in a field placement at Pierce SEd where they would learn specifically how to develop, teach in and manage their own programs. The students, CTP graduates once they had completed the quarter and met the essential functions of the job while in the placement, would become SEd Coordinators in their home areas. They would then have ongoing access to technical assistance and support from the Partnership. Thus, SEd programs would multiply across the state, people with psychiatric disabilities would have access to responsible employment positions and SEd students would be served by people who have the skills and passion to help others with these disabilities reach their educational goals.

Wells-Moran negotiated the beginning of another SEd program in Thurston-Mason RSN, Olympia, as part of her role with the CTP. A student was trained by the CTP and Pierce SEd, and then became the Coordinator there. Braedt developed a *Supported Education Field Placement Curriculum* to ensure that coordinators in training there would be well prepared to operate programs essentially on their own. The next year, programs were initiated in Longview-Kelso, twin cities in Southwest RSN, and Mt. Vernon, North Sound RSN.

In 1998, it became clear to the Partners that increased structure to their technical assistance and support services was needed. That year, an MHD contract addendum to the CTP for the work of the Partnership included the writing of a manual for use by the SEd programs. This became a central organizing tool. While the contract included the work already underway, the Manual idea was raised and included in the contract by Marianne Neff-Daniels, at the MHD.

The Evergreen State College, also in Thurston-Mason RSN, agreed to try a CTP student in a field placement there in 2000, with the idea of possible future development of a full SEd Program. The Evergreen State College Supported Education services were never fully developed and Capital Clubhouse, in the same city, plans to serve those students through the Clubhouse's Supported Education function. The Longview-Kelso Supported Education Program has moved most functions to a local community services agency and the Program will serve people with other disabilities, as well as people with psychiatric disabilities. This approach is discussed briefly in the Manual as an option for rural areas.

Two new programs have been initiated for 2002. Again, two or more CTP students will be trained in the CTP and Pierce SEd, and then will become Coordinators. The Partnership holds monthly support and assistance meetings and provides support and technical assistance by phone and in person, as needed. Occasionally, more formal trainings are held in those meetings, as well.

Documents in the Manual can be individualized for the particular setting, program design and other factors that make each program unique. While there are other models of Supported Education, the Partnership has primarily helped to develop college-based programs, for the normalizing and natural environment, ease of student movement into regular, integrated, college classes, convenience of students and access to college resources. Where the Partnership helped develop Supported Education in a clubhouse setting, use of college facilities for the Support Group and links to departments and people at the college site remain important.

The Partnership recognizes that users of the Manual will choose or be required to fashion it according to individual circumstances. The Manual is not only a policies and procedures text, nor is it a complete instruction book on developing SEd Programs. It is also incomplete concerning the training of Coordinators or educating Supervisors on their roles. It is, however, a helpful tool for operating a Program. It includes information on program development, a program description, mission and models, personnel and administrative materials, marketing and forming alliances, program content, consumers as coordinators, resources for SEd students and a bibliography. In other words, it contains what was most needed by SEd Coordinators, their Supervisors and their Advisory Boards in our experience over the past few years. The Partnership sincerely hopes that new users will also find it very helpful.

The Need

Many people who have psychiatric disabilities have had their education delayed or interrupted by their disorders or because of other reasons. People with psychiatric disabilities can succeed with educational aspirations, but many need support and assistance.

History of Supported Education

Karen Unger, M.S.W., Ed.D, began Supported Education at Boston University in 1983, following the psychiatric rehabilitation values and philosophies about which Bill Anthony, Ph.D., at Boston U., had been writing. Unger developed college preparatory courses and student support groups. Unger affirmed anecdotal Supported Education success stories with research that began generating Supported Education programs, in various forms, across the country.

What the Partnership Does

- Initiates idea of Supported Education with colleges, mental health funders and administrators, consumer groups and mental health agencies;
- Assists in planning;
- Helps with selection and trains potential coordinators;
- Provides ongoing technical assistance and support to coordinators and technical assistance to supervisors, advisory boards and funders;
- Advocates for coordinators' needs as employees with their supervisors and funders;
- Provides this generic manual of policies, procedures, start-up schedules, job descriptions, forms and information to be individualized by program coordinators.

What a Supported Education Program Can Do

Help adults with psychiatric disabilities:

- Decide upon education and career goals;
- Develop skills and *confidence*;
- Learn about and prepare for GED, adult basic education or college-level courses and provide support for success;
- Navigate the college assessment, application, registration, and financial aid processes;

- Learn to use campus resources;
- Negotiate reasonable accommodations for the disability in school.

The Barriers

- Old beliefs of case managers and other mental health service providers concerning the intellectual capacities of people who have psychiatric disorders;
- Outdated concerns of mental health service providers about a need to protect consumers of services from the stresses of being in school and working;
- Mistaken beliefs of educational institution personnel that students with psychiatric disorders will be disruptive on campus;
- False notions of educational institution personnel about the costs of providing accommodations to students with psychiatric disorders;
- Limited knowledge of mental health funders and agency administrators concerning the effects of education on the lives of people who have psychiatric disorders;
- Lack of understanding by mental health personnel of no-cost or low cost educational financing, the role of campus disabilities specialists;
- The ADA as it pertains to education and reasonable accommodations that work in the classroom and the benefits of peer-student support on campus.

Basics of Structure

- Assessment and admission based on student interest(s) and choice(s);
- College classroom for preparatory classes, usually with only other students who have psychiatric disabilities;
- Set curriculum to include goal setting and college preparatory information and skills development;
- No grades;
- Course work is self-paced and students may re-take courses;
- No fee to students;
- Student support group when enrolled in college courses;
- One-to-one individualized assistance;
- Access for consumers of mental health services and other adults with psychiatric disabilities to public secondary education;
- Assist consumers of mental health services and other adults with psychiatric disabilities to develop educational goals and plans to meet those goals;
- Support consumers of mental health services and other adults with psychiatric disabilities to reach their educational goals;
- Help build natural support systems through the process of accessing and participating in education.

What Do Supported Education Programs Actually do?

Through classroom, individual and, sometimes, workshop processes:

- Most programs help their students decide upon education and job goals;
- Most programs offer college preparatory classes or workshops on study and test-taking skills;
- Most programs provide tours of the campus(es);
- Most programs offer individualized assistance with the college entrance assessment office, registration office, disabilities office, advising office and financial aid office, and advocate for students as needed;
- Most programs provide information on GED preparation, adult basic education courses, college-level courses and other educational opportunities;
- Most programs teach students how to identify and negotiate needed and reasonable accommodations, allowed under the Americans with Disabilities Act (ADA), for the disability in school;
- Most programs teach students how to fill out college forms and obtain supportive resources such as transportation;
- Most programs maintain communication with mental health service providers, college disabilities specialists and instructors to ensure SEd and college access to potential students and collaborative relationships to support current students;

- Most programs provide student support groups and provide links to various community resources.

What are the Outcomes of Supported Education Programs in Washington State?

- Five Supported Education programs run by part or full-time Coordinators who have Psychiatric Disabilities themselves
  - one program in a clubhouse
  - three programs in community colleges (one now operated through a community action agency with links to the college)
  - one program in a state college (no longer in operation, but campus outreach from the clubhouse is planned)

- Two new Supported Education programs run by part-time Coordinators who have psychiatric disabilities themselves are planned

In Washington state, over a two-year period:

- About 50% of Supported Education students per year dropped the first time around from those programs before completing the college preparation classes;

- Yet, an average of 50% of those students who dropped per year, either went to work or into college courses without further Supported Education or Supported Employment;

- Figures for later return of students who left the programs before completion averaged approximately 50% per year;

- About 10% of students repeated the same Supported Education college preparatory courses;

- One half-time coordinator has been able to serve up to approximately 30 different students in a month when the program was held at one central site, without any other staff assistance;

- From Supported Education, about 13% of students took adult basic education courses, 13% of Supported Education students took GED courses, 64% took college level courses and 10% took specific vocational training courses—17% per year graduated with a 2 or 4-yr. college degree or certificate;

- The average rate of student satisfaction with Supported Education programs in Washington has been 95%.

What Are the Outcomes of Supported Education Programs Elsewhere?

- Studies at Thresholds in Chicago and the University of Arizona have reported 47% and 41% of former Supported Education students working after participation in Supported Education (Weisburd, 1997);

- The U. Arizona study reported 54% of students who were in or completed Supported Education in a 6-year period were enrolled in college level courses (Weisburd, 1997);

- In one study, the only differences found in the resources needed to provide accommodations between a group of students with psychiatric disabilities and a group of students with other disabilities was greater need for more personal support by the group with psychiatric disabilities—U. Arizona (Weisburd, 1997);

- These and other studies report that students with psychiatric disabilities tend to have higher grade point averages than other students, the retention rates tend to be about the same as for other students and demographics are reported to be comparable, with the exception of age;

- The average age has been found to be 40 years for students with psychiatric disabilities returning to college, compared to 33 years for others returning to college (Weisburd, 1997);
- Compared to community support participants, some indication has been found that students who enter Supported Education tend to have higher education backgrounds and more recent employment histories, diagnoses seem to be spread evenly in Supported Education programs and Supported Education students may tend to historically have higher rates of hospitalization and issues with medications (Weisburd, 1997).

Other Frequent Results of Supported Education Observed

- Increased eye contact, posture, neatness, assertiveness;
- Self-reports of greater self-care, confidence, meaning, self-knowledge, hope, and sense of achievement and life direction;
- Inspiration to other people with psychiatric disabilities;
- Improved relationships with family members;
- New friendships;
- Increased planning skills;
- Increased participation in a community;
- New self-respect.

CHAPTER 1

DESCRIPTION OF A SUPPORTED EDUCATION PROGRAM

Mission

The mission of a supported education program is to support, assist and improve educational access and progress to persons with psychiatric disabilities in the continuation of their recovery. Karen Unger (1991) describes the mission of Supported Education as providing education in integrated settings for individuals with severe psychiatric disabilities for whom post-secondary education has been interrupted or intermittent as a result of their disability. Many individuals with these disabilities need ongoing support services to be successful in the educational environment.

Supported Education offers vocational and social opportunities for consumers to develop and pursue goals in a normalized and non-stigmatizing setting.

Supported Education Coordinator, Lynn Braedt, describes the mission as:

- Assisting the consumer in the recovery process through meaningful community education activities;

- Ensuring opportunities for individuals with psychiatric disabilities to achieve their educational goals and to improve their vocational options;
- Offering classes to prepare the individual for post-secondary education and providing necessary ongoing support;
- Assisting in the adjustment to a college campus, providing linkages to other campus services, and assisting in negotiating college systems;
- Advocating for removal of barriers;
- Providing assistance in obtaining accommodations;
- Teaching self-advocacy skills, providing information to empower consumers;
- Increasing the college community's understanding of and ability to educationally support college students with psychiatric disabilities.

Supported Education reduces exposure to stigma, self-designated stigma, and isolation for participants. It also increases self-confidence, self-determination and improves self-identity.

Goals and Outcomes

Supported Education is a significant option for consumers that is interrelated to, and consistent with, the recovery process. SEd meets outcomes that include:

- Meeting consumers' preferences for non-stigmatizing service delivery;

- Participation in classes, to work on their goals, in a normalized setting;
- Increased vocational and social opportunities and choices;
- Choices of and preparation for successfully continuing education;
- Development of natural and normalized supports;
- Opportunities for positive interactions between the consumer and the community as a way to decrease stigma and increase campus diversity mandates;
- Increased use of community-based resources.

Ishmaels' Story

Ishmael had lived with his family in this country for almost 8 years, but he is still had a heavy accent and understood only some of what was said to him in English. He could read or write almost no English. At 24 years of age, he couldn't fill out a job application, let alone understand everything a supervisor would need to tell him on the job. His parents had allowed Ishmael to remain living in their home and spoke little English inside the home. His mother explained to the Supported Education Coordinator that Ishmael had spent most of almost 5 years in bed and would often seem "gone," not speaking to anyone and staring into space.

At the urging of a family friend, Ishmael began seeing a psychiatrist about one year ago and began taking medications for depression. His mother explained that he wasn't oversleeping as much and now went out on errands for the household. Since he had been interested in a college education when he was younger, she was urging him to participate in "this program the doctor told me of." Ishmael agreed to meet with the Supported Education Coordinator.

With help from the Coordinator and the English-as-a-Second Language Program on campus, Ishmael became enrolled in their English courses and attended faithfully. The Coordinator met with him every other week for half an hour or so to encourage Ishmael and see his progress. Six months later, he asked to take the Supported Education Campus Orientation Course, and then finished all of the Supported Education courses.

He was excited to then take the college courses he had always dreamed of, biology and math. He was very proud, held his head high these days and looked people in the eye. Although he still struggled with the language, he studied hard and made progress.

In three years, Ishmael graduated from the community college with an Associate's Degree in Science (AS) and was accepted at the University of California where he would major in pre-med. His ultimate goal was to become a physician's assistant and he felt sure this was a reasonable goal. He knew he had to take medications for his depression, stay in touch with his friends and let his doctor know when he had trouble sleeping. He also knew that he could handle no more than three courses at any one time, two if one was an advanced math course.

Ishmael was physically active, working out three times per week, and had learned this was a part of keeping himself healthy. His family agreed to pay for a dorm room and campus meals. He was on his way.

The Supported Education Coordinator hears from Ishmael from time to time and sometimes helps him sort out what he happens to be struggling with at the time, usually maintaining a regular schedule and making it to his classes when he feels down. There was one period of three months during which Ishmael moved home after a hospitalization. Yet, he had learned not to let his disorder stop him and he re-entered college the next quarter, taking two rather light load courses while regaining his health. During that hospitalization, Ishmael was able to tell hospital staff that he had didn't get along with one of his professors and started skipping the classes. He then began having sleep problems and stopped attending both classes.

Yet, he had learned from Supported Education that he should drop the courses, and he did, so that he would not receive failing grades. He then hid out in his dorm room, often sleeping over 20 hours per day. His parents, worried, had visited and had him hospitalized. He had stopped taking his medications by that time.

Although it took Ishmael some time to regain his footing, he moved back to the dorms, continued in college, graduated with a Bachelor's in Science (BS) and was accepted at the University's medical school. He is now finishing his second year of medical school and has an apartment where he lives with his girlfriend of two years. He plans to work part-time, at first, as a physician's assistant after he graduates.

Supported Education Models

Varied models of Supported Education have been developed nationwide. Combinations of the following basic forms, identified by K. Unger (1991), have emerged:

- Self-Contained: Students attend classes on a post-secondary site with other students who have psychiatric disabilities. The curriculum is set and students receive the same instruction in the same classroom. The students are not initially integrated into regular classes, but they may participate in activities and use the resources of the institution. Support is available from program staff for students as they progress and move into regular classes. Program staff may be from the sponsoring organization and/or from the academic institution.

- On-site: Students attend regular classes at the post-secondary site. Support is provided by the staff from the post-secondary site where consumers are matriculated and receive credit. Services are most often provided through disabled student services or mental health/counseling services on campus.

- Mobile Support: This model is the same as the on site model, except that the support is provided by staff from community based mental health services or rehabilitation programs.

While each model has its strengths, most programs tend to combine or adapt these models. For example, a Supported Education program may provide self-contained preparation classes in order to eventually integrate students into regular classes, as in the on-site support model. Support may be provided by community based mental health personnel, who coordinate and team with college disabilities services to provide support and accommodations.

It is part of the role of a Supported Education coordinator to assist the consumer-student in identifying and obtaining needed accommodations. Accommodations most frequently requested by Supported Education participants are:

- Assistance with registration and financial aid;
- Extended time on exams;
- Change of locations for exams;
- Priority parking;
- Note taking, tape recorders;
- Seating arrangement modifications;
- Beverages in class;
- Peer support;
- Identified place to meet on campus that is non-threatening before or after class;

- Incompletes rather than failures if relapse occurs;
- Training in time management;
- Training in study skills;
- Assistance in goal setting;
- Special topics courses;
- Understanding of psychiatric disorders as they affect various individuals.

Tom's Story

Tom had been served in the Community Support Program for 6 years when he heard about Supported Education through a poster at the mental health center. He had worked part-time as a gas station attendant for 2 years of his time receiving psychiatric and case management services at the mental health center. This was a job he had gotten himself through a friend of his father's. After two years, though, he felt he would like to do something other than his work at the gas station, but he wasn't sure what he would like to do. One day, in frustration with his job, he quit and went to the mental health center to find out if there were other options he could seek for employment.

In discussing his frustration with his job with his Case Manager, Tom explained he had grown bored and felt he wanted to pursue employment where he felt better fulfilled and might even be better paid. The Case Manager worked for several months with Tom to search for an employment position Tom could find meaningful. Nothing seemed to match his skills and interests well enough.

Tom had graduated from high school and worked for three years in automotive repair when he became ill in his early twenties. He was then unemployed for three years. That was before his gas station job.

The Case Manager had just decided Tom was being unrealistic about his employment expectations when Tom pointed out the Supported Education poster to her. Tom decided, with the encouragement of his Case Manager and the Supported Education Coordinator, to pursue the idea of further education that might lead to a more rewarding career. In his first meeting with Supported Education Coordinator at his local community college, Tom was impressed that the Coordinator stated that she, too, was a consumer of mental health services, but his sprits sank as he realized that even this person who had this level of responsibility, was still receiving mental health services. He had hoped to put that aspect of his life behind him.

Tom decided he would attend the Orientation course and see what it felt like and what he could gain from it. He felt very confused about what he should take in college and even if he was going to be able to go into college courses or handle them. Maybe he would get some answers through this course.

Two months later, Tom had completed the Orientation course and was beginning to identify what he really wanted in his career and to learn the courses he would need to take to get there. The Supported Education Coordinator had helped him realize how much he cared about animals by doing some interest inventories with him. She had also helped him understand how to ask for accommodations in the classroom and job so that when he felt symptomatic, he could take a break without losing his place in a college course.

Tom also learned where to go on the college campus to find out what courses he might take that would lead to a job working with animals—to an academic counselor. The academic counselor and the Supported Education Coordinator encouraged Tom to complete the Supported Education courses, while registering for the next quarter to take one course.

Tom loved being in class, but was taken aback by all of the homework required for just one course! He had wanted to take four courses! Now, he was glad that he hadn't. The Supported Education Coordinator had visited the Disabilities Office on campus and the staff person there had agreed that the college could grant an accommodation to Tom to spread out the assignment expectations over the quarter. He didn't have to use the other accommodation, the one asking for a break without consequences if he became symptomatic.

The Disabilities Specialist wrote a letter to the course Instructor explaining that assignments needed to be spread more evenly over the quarter for Tom because of his disability. Tom felt overwhelmed with so many expectations all at once and would begin to back away unless he could break the work down into parts to be tackled one at a time. He had not mastered that yet, so the Supported Education Coordinator was instrumental in explaining it to the Disabilities Specialist. The Coordinator thought that, perhaps, for the next course, Tom could do this for himself. This became one of his goals in the Supported Education Program.

Three times during his college life, Tom's Supported Education peers in the Support Group encouraged him to cut back and to use his accommodations. Once, one of the group members even went to his house to tell him how much they had missed him at the last Group meeting, as Tom had been isolating again — not attending the Group and missing several of his college classes. The Coordinator convinced him he needn't drop from college when he received only a C grade, after he said he was leaving college because he just couldn't do all of the homework. The next quarter, he was back on track working with the Coordinator to break his homework into small parts and tackle each, one at a time.

Tom finished the course with a B+ average and was thrilled at the grade and his direction. Over the next year or so, Tom did learn to break down course assignments into smaller parts and began taking two and then three courses per quarter. At two and one-half years, Tom graduated with a two-year vocational training certificate in Veterinary Assistance. His family, several friends, Supported Education classmates, the Supported Education

Coordinator and the Disabilities Specialist gave a loud group cheer at graduation when Tom was handed his Certificate.

It took Tom three interviews and two months, but he has now been in his job, and says he loves it, for over one year. Now, when new people ask what he does, he tells them with pride and a feeling of accomplishment. Sometimes, he really forgets to tell them he has a psychiatric disability. He just doesn't think about being a consumer anymore, except when he goes to have his prescription refilled.

CHAPTER 2

SUPPORTED EDUCATION PROGRAM DEVELOPMENT

The Pleasures, Perils and Unpredictability of Planning

Planning is usually not linear, as most planning texts report, and as anyone who has been involved in program planning knows, it can often be rewarding, frustrating, enjoyable, maddening, disappointing, straightforward and chaotic. You are provided here with something like a map for planning a Supported Education program that we hope you'll find helpful. We found out by just plunging in that these were the elements, more or less in order, of planning for the programs with which we've been involved. In hindsight, we could have avoided some of the perils we suffered as a result of not adopting a planning model earlier, but we're now using the following model to provide guidelines for the process. Again, planning is not usually linear in practice, so keep flexibility in mind.

Supported Education in Rural Areas

SEd programs sometimes, by necessity, serve program participants with other disabilities too. This is most frequently done in rural areas where resources are few. A Supported Education coordinator in this kind of program may feel less knowledgeable about other disability groups besides those with psychiatric disabilities, yet the values and principles inherent to SEd models are applicable to other disability groups and their needs as well. The organization of such a diverse SEd program may differ somewhat from other SEd model programs.

Many people with disabilities will have experienced issues in meeting their educational goals and most will need advocacy and support. People with other disabilities need to become aware of accommodations that will assist them in reaching their educational goals too. In some cases, support groups may be offered specific to type of disability. More typically, many people with disabilities have similar challenges and can benefit from each others' experiences. When working with a person with a disability unfamiliar to the coordinator, it's always advisable to search out literature and resource people concerning the effects of the disability on learning in order to discover what particular approaches may be most helpful in the SEd program. Additional, or different, resources may also be available to the student with a disability other than psychiatric disability.

Figure 2:1. Supported Education Program Initiation Steps:

Assess Need, Involving Key Mental Health and Education People
Research and Identify Supported Education Program Models
Compile List of Resources Needed
Identify College Contribution Possibilities

Identify Major Funding Source(s)

Develop Program/Staffing/Marketing Plan, and Proposed Budget

Determine Office Location and Supervisor

Establish Funding and Other Resource Contributions for:

- coordinator pay
- college or other office space
- classroom space
- supervision
- telephone, computer, desk, filing cabinet, copier
- clerical support
- office and classroom supplies

Hire Coordinator and Train Supervisor and Coordinator

Develop Advisory Board

Initiation Steps

Step 1: Assess Need, Involving Key Mental Health and Education People

- Funders may well want some indication of whether people with psychiatric disabilities in their service area would use Supported Education;

- Involving people who use services, from the outset of planning, is good practice;
- Collaboration between key mental health and education people may be needed to make sure SEd students have access to college services and resources;
- Funding and in-kind contributions to an SEd program often require both mental health and college resources;
- Primary stakeholders often support projects they've helped to develop;
- Mental health agencies may help make people they serve to become aware of SEd as a resource if they understand and feel some sense of ownership in the Program.

Step 2: Research and Identify Supported Education Program Models

- The models discussed in the literature, including the pros and cons of each model, should be presented to the initial stakeholder group;
- Stakeholders need to know what the choices are, what outcomes and issues each model may present, and why you may prefer one model over others: This is part of establishing buy-in and critical to avoiding later misunderstandings about how the program should be operated;
- Some models may be better suited to; the circumstances of the local area, the stakeholder constituency, existing resources, and the ability and willingness of potential funders to contribute financially.

Step 3: Compile List of Resources Needed

- Once the model has been identified, the resources that will be needed for the SEd program become more apparent;
- A process of thinking through what will be needed and talking with others who've developed such programs should enable the stakeholders, or a leader, to compile a realistic list of major needs;
- It's always important to include location of an office and classroom, supplies, reasonable coordinator pay, a supervisor or mentor, and equipment (computer, copier, telephone), on this list;
- The group or leader may need to go back to the drawing board more than once on this list and may even find they need to approach other potential funders, especially if the people who can help financially in the stakeholders group are objecting.

Step 4: Identify College Contribution Possibilities

- Colleges often find it easier to contribute space, use of equipment and, sometimes, supervision or mentorship, than funding;
- A college may be short on space, but alternatives are to hold classes late in the afternoon and share a part-time staff office;
- Another alternative is to hold the classes and site the office at a location very near to the college, so the coordinator can accompany students on tours and to various offices and students can easily get from the college to the program;
- Some programs provide transportation to a college(s) instead of being located on campus, or the site may be easily accessi-

ble by public transportation or within walking distance of the campus;

- Programs not located on campus can arrange tours, meetings with campus personnel, as needed, and a space for the student support group on campus.

Step 5: Identify Major Funding Source(s)

- Probably by this stage, there has already been some discussion concerning who will pay for the coordinator wages, supplies and perhaps even some or all equipment;

- State mental health, regional and provider agencies are the most likely to finance such programs, but short-term or pilot grants should not be overlooked if there is some assurance of funding down the road beyond the grant time period;

- Many states have consumer-operated programs and projects that can be accessed through proposal writing;

- Funding may be administered through the college, a consumer organization, an advocacy association, a mental health agency, a regional mental health administration, an affiliated provider agency, or even be contracted directly with the SEd program or coordinator;

- Supervision, or mentorship, may be provided by an experienced supervisor or mentor at the college, a consumer-operated association, community service agency or program, regional mental health system or local mental health agency.

Step 6: Develop Program/Staffing/Marketing Plan, and Proposed Budget

- Write a plan that includes a brief description of the program's purpose, constituency and location;
- Also include how it will be staffed: This will depend on the number of people your group would like the program to serve and the model you choose;
- Remember that if the program is in a college setting, work-study students and later, graduates of the program, may be excellent part-time staff who can be of great help to the Coordinator;
- The Partnership for Development of Supported Education believes, again, that a person who has experienced the mental health system, a psychiatric disorder, is very interested in the coordinator position, is in recovery and meets the hiring requirements for the particular model, brings a special sense of understanding, motivation and knowledge of resources to the job;
- Requirements for the Coordinator position should include some college experience as a student, training or experience in program management and working with people who have psychiatric disorders, the ability to establish rapport with students, basic understanding of SEd and capacity for training or teaching;
- Write position requirements into the plan;
- Include how the Coordinator will be mentored or supervised, supported and trained in operating a Supported Education Program in the plan;

- Identify the general marketing and consumer constituencies ahead of time, in the plan;
- Research and develop an initial budget for the plan that covers estimated costs of supplies and salary (ies);
- Develop alternatives for the above categories, in case the groups' first choices are not possible;
- A good plan always includes measurable goals and/or objectives, strategies, designation of who is responsible and deadlines for completion of tasks.

Step 7: Determine Office Location and Supervisor

- It's time to make some final decisions and firm up the plan by first strategizing to attain any needed agreements, particularly concerning location and identity of the supervisor or mentor.

Step 8: Establish Funding and Other Resource Contributions for: coordinator pay; college or other office space; classroom space supervision; telephone, computer, desk, filing cabinet, copier clerical support; office and classroom supplies.

- The major effort is almost over on this project once you've established who will pay for what and how much each will pay;
- In negotiating who will pay and how much, it will be necessary to present your plan clearly and simply and describe the benefits to funders you are approaching, unless all of the necessary funding representatives are in the planning group.

Step 9: Hire Coordinator and Train Supervisor and Coordinator

- The process may actually be reversed from hiring, then training, to training, then hiring, as it is in Washington State where candidates are identified, trained and hired if they've met the essential functions of the position on the field placement;

- While this works well in Washington, because we have a consumer-provider (prosumer) training program and now a field placement training site, others where these resources do not exist may want to design a training curriculum that includes contact with other SEd coordinators elsewhere and specific literature to be read, once the coordinator has been hired;

- Coordinators from other areas of the country may also be sent to Washington State for training through the Partnership or the Partnership will train at your site;

- Your group, or perhaps by this time, the funder or supervisor, may decide to initiate a prosumer training program also, so that future SEd programs can also be developed following the Partnership model in Washington. Thus, consumers have better chances at many types of mental health employment success.

Step 10: Develop Advisory Board

- Some of the initial planning group may want to serve on the new program's advisory board;

- The roles and constituency of the advisory board are discussed later (Section V—Personnel);

- Most of the development of the board should be left to the Coordinator as she or he will know best who needs to be brought into the loop, who will provide needed input and who, from the planning group, needs to be involved.

College Organizational Structure: Department Descriptions

While every four-year college, technical school and community college is organized to meet the goals and functions of that individual institution, there are departments and organizational components typical to most college campuses. These are usually called something close to the following; Student Services, Administrative Services, Institutional Technology and Continuing Education.

Student Services

Campuses consist of divisions of academic studies, such as Business, Arts and Humanities, Social Sciences and Technology, as well as services, such as Registration, Advising, Counseling, Testing and Assessment and Disabilities Support. Each division has instructors who teach, and staff who support the functions of the particular division. A division may include, in some cases, a variety of content areas. For example, a division may include high school completion, study skills, adult basic education and high school equivalency test preparation courses.

Advising and Registration

The advising system is designed to help students develop plans of course work to meet career or academic needs. The Advising Center can also assist in the registration process.

Financial Aid

Financial assistance is often available from varying sources, particularly for people with disabilities. Aid is awarded according to state, federal and college guidelines. Becoming familiar with these guidelines is helpful for prospective Supported Education students.

Disability Support Services (DSS)

Supported Education Coordinators work closely with DSS. When a Supported Education student desires accommodations, the Disabilities Office can often provide a liaison to instructors, specialized assistance, equipment and other resources. Students typically need to bring documentation of the disability with them to a meeting with DSS and the meeting should be planned far enough ahead of time to allow DSS staff to arrange accommodations. SEd Coordinators often accompany their students to such meetings. The working relationship between the Supported Education Coordinator and this service is ideally strong.

Tutorial Services

SEd students can use these services for help with college courses.

Administrative Services

This organizational component of the college includes payroll, bookstore, food services, security, accounting, human resources, purchasing, print shop, parking, and sometimes other functions. Most fiscal operations are carried out within these services.

Institutional Technology

While Supported Education Coordinators may not regularly interact with this component of the organization, technology, telecommunications, staff computers, computer labs for students and, especially, distance learning provides resources and choices for all students.

Continuing Education/Extended Learning/Contracted Education/Lifelong Learning

This part of the organization generally includes all classes offered to the community at large, contracted courses for specialty populations, and professional training and vocational and technical programs. Supported Education is often a part of the Continuing Education Department.

Career/Work First

This department is available for career counseling, interest inventories and career assessment. These resources should be an integral part of a comprehensive Supported Education Program.

Library

The campus library, or learning center, has a broad spectrum of available technologies with essential information available. Most students will strongly depend on library resources in order to complete homework assignments for college courses.

Strategies for Successful Inclusion of Persons with Mental Illness on College Campuses

Administrators

- Know and follow ADA/accommodations/law;
- Initiate Supported Education programs or elements of same;
- Provide adequate staff training regarding diagnosis, symptoms and how to help the student though comment and referral;
- Provide clear policies and procedures;
- Institute peer counseling or mechanism for counseling support;
- Identify ways for students to obtain skills with more flexible funding support;
- Allow liberal use of incompletes;
- Investigate computer technology for classroom alternative learning (distance learning);
- Initiate and support stronger emphasis of special populations (person with psychiatric disabilities) in cultural diversity trainings.

Faculty

- Work cooperatively with Supported Education programs and Special Needs Coordinators;
- Increase abilities to teach all learning styles;

- Increase experiential learning opportunities;
- Develop basic understanding of persons with psychiatric disabilities;
- Be prepared to set behavioral limits as identified in college policy (Student Handbook);
- Increase use of appropriate and varied teaching strategies;
- Be able to interact and attempt to achieve degree of rapport with student;
- Know campus mental health resources and how to access;
- Know how to teach subject area to persons at varied points of academic skill spectrum;
- Work cooperatively with student to support accommodations;
- Embrace diversity to include persons with a psychiatric disability.

Disabilities Coordinators

- Work cooperatively with Supported Education personnel;
- Recognize and respect issues of confidentiality and limits to histories and other personal information shared;
- Avoid becoming a therapist or case manager;
- Know community and campus mental health resources and how to access if no Supported Education program exists on campus;

- Recognize what is truly disruptive in class and what is not (e.g., sleeping in class) and be willing to communicate the same to faculty;

- Recognize the need for varied accommodations and a "set" of accommodations that are appropriate to persons with cognitive disorders.

Students

- Participate in the process of identifying accommodations;

- Know College policies (rules) and follow them;

- Use Supported Education program and other support resources;

- Work at maintaining mental health.

Typical Program Start-Up

It is necessary to lay the foundation for a SEd program by starting with prospective student meetings with the coordinator(s), the orientation course and, perhaps then, the student support group. The first meeting for assessment of an applicant's initial goals, expectations and needs help potential students decide whether Supported Education is the path they need and want to take. Sometimes, the process takes more than one meeting. This is usually called the student intake process.

This intake process will help the coordinator determine if the program is the best option for the particular student. The coordinator may make other recommendations to applicants that are better suited to them, although applicants who want to participate are not denied the opportunity. The coordinator may make the recommendation that an enrolled student simply participate in the support group or start with a particular course later. The coordinator will also need to plan for the provision of adequate support and resources for each student.

The orientation course should be taken first in most cases, except when a student is already taking courses on campus and is already familiar with the information offered in that course. This means implementation of the SEd curriculum usually needs to begin with this course.

A further scenario for effective start-up may be the following: Once the first orientation course has ended, the next course should begin for that first group, but the orientation course can begin again with a new group and any students wanting to take it again or to take missed class sessions the first time around. Once the second course has ended, the third can begin. At the end of the third, a fourth course can begin. It is usually necessary to offer the orientation course each quarter, since new students will be more likely to stay with the program if they don't have to wait months to begin.

It's important to start slowly with courses in the first several months. This will give the coordinator time to market the program to potential students and their support service providers. Incremental start-up is helpful to the coordinator who will need the time to become familiar with the first group of students and subsequent applicants and students. Consideration of the particular needs of the students involved takes time and development of the upcoming courses and preparation for providing those courses will result in a better program.

If the coordinator is overwhelmed at the outset because she or he is trying to teach most or all of the courses, program quality will suffer. The coordinator must have the time for the support group. In the first year, in particular, new students will be the norm and most will need to make a connection with the coordinator at the beginning of their involvement with the program. New students who make that personal connection with the coordinator are most likely to stay in the program.

The coordinator will also need to learn the ins and outs of the particular college and become acquainted with key personnel on campus in the first months. After all, coordinators must have current and thorough campus and resource information and many relationships with personnel in varying departments and offices for program effectiveness. Program coordinators, especially at the beginning of the new program, also need to spend time getting to know key staff people in the mental health agencies and, perhaps, in other organizations serving people with psychiatric disabilities. These are tasks that can take significant time and shouldn't be relegated to a few minutes here and there because the coordinator is trying to offer everything at once. (See the Policy and Procedure for Intake and Assessment in Section III for further information on that process.)

Curriculum Development

Supported Education Programs often have differing components and courses. The teaching materials for each of the courses will need to be specific to that program and its participants. However, there are curricula already developed and available from several sources. The Partnership and the Center for Psychiatric Recovery and Rehabilitation Education have developed some useful resources for Supported Education courses. Individual coordinators have also developed materials for their programs.

Some materials have been borrowed and may have been adapted to the needs of a particular program. Most college bookstores have textbooks that may be drawn from for specific lessons and all departments, offices and divisions will have written materials pertaining to information needed by SEd students. The Internet and resources at libraries may be helpful on some topics too.

While the Supported Education Coordinator is not expected to be a writer of all original curricula (this skill is not common to all teachers or group facilitators), it is helpful that a coordinator be resourceful by collecting materials on topics to be covered in the courses. Look for materials that offer information on;

- Campus resources
- Financial Aid
- Parking regulations
- Student responsibilities
- Admissions
- Registration
- Grading
- Accessing tutors
- Study habits and skills
- ADA and accommodations
- Time Management
- Note-taking
- Listening skills
- Test-taking
- Writing papers
- Career Exploration
- Goal development
- Job readiness
- Self-esteem
- Building support
- Stigma and barriers
- Self-disclosure
- Symptom management
- Stress and school
- Motivation

Interaction with other Supported Education coordinators is an ideal way to compare and develop materials for teaching, as well. Individual coordinators for SEd courses can do the development of lessons for teaching, should the time, interest and skill be available to the coordinator. Again, not everyone likes or feels comfortable with this task. However, the lesson plan form included in this Manual is an available blueprint for developing your own curricula and lessons.

Teri's Story

Teri told a friend that she would do anything to finish high school, to get her GED, if only she thought she could really do it. She had tried twice before, at her local community college. The friend told her she might get some help from the Supported Education Program that had begun last year at the college. The friend explained something of how it works and Teri decided to go see them.

Teri was very nervous when she met the Coordinator at the Supported Education Program that week. She was shown around the Supported Education rooms, where students seemed to be hard at work on computers and reading and writing. The Coordinator encouraged Teri to return for an appointment to talk about what she would like from Supported Education in some further detail and was given a time. Teri did not show for the appointment and when she told her friend, the friend said she would help her make a call to reschedule and even go to the appointment with her. Teri decided, at the college on her appointment day, that she could go into the appointment herself after all.

She came out smiling and told her friend she thought this would work out fine. She had a class schedule for the Supported Education Orientation Course and would begin the next week.

Teri did well in the Supported Education courses, but was still very fearful of the GED courses. Another student volunteered to go into that first class with her. The Coordinator volunteered to talk with the Instructor with Teri beforehand and to help her register for the course. Although Teri sometimes lost heart during the course, she did complete all of the preparatory work to take the GED tests. She also attended two more courses in the Supported Education Program and began planning for the possibility of taking a college course, English 101, as she had always liked to read and knew she needed to write better for the kind of secretarial work she hoped to get in the future.

Then, Teri refused to come to the college for the GED tests. She also wouldn't do the tests from a computer in the Supported

Education Program. The Coordinator made a couple of calls to encourage Teri to return, but Teri refused and would not discuss it. Teri received a letter from the Coordinator assuring her that she would be welcome to return to Supported Education at any time in the future and, whether she chose to take the tests or develop another educational goal, the Program was still open to her. Four months later, Teri returned, took the Supported Education Goal-Setting Course again, and decided to take the GED tests. The Coordinator helped her brush-up by assigning GED study reviews and soon Teri made the appointment for testing and received the GED Certificate.

Teri announced the next Monday that she would be registering for English 101 for the next college quarter and set an appointment time with the Coordinator to register and to apply for financial aid to cover the cost of the course. One year later, the Coordinator attended Teri's graduation where Teri received a one-year secretarial certificate. She had already interviewed for two part-time jobs and the Vocational Counselor at her mental health center had spoken with Teri and the Coordinator on how best to support Teri in getting a job and maintaining it.

Budget Tips

This section is included to give the reader an idea of approximate line item amounts when developing a Supported Education Program budget. Estimated costs can be extrapolated from the figures here, according to the number of students to be served. The format of the primary funding or site organization is usually applied and SEd Coordinators usually have assistance from a supervisor, funding representative or someone in the business department in completing a budget. The following costs will usually be associated with operation of a Supported Education Program.

Salaries and Wages

Coordinators tend to earn entry level, BA equivalent, mental health field wages or salaries. Within any state, this may vary from area to area. The average pay to beginning Coordinators in Washington State is approximately $13 per hour, before taxes. At this rate of pay, a half-time Coordinator would earn $13,052 per year. Work study matching for college student help can be as low as half of the local minimum wage per hour. Assistants whose duties involve basic clerical tasks may earn the minimum or up to $9.00 per hour, depending on the local market and the organization's pay scale for equal work. Assistants whose duties are, at least in part, working directly with students usually earn more. Salaries should rise to a better living wage as staff gain experience on the job.

Personnel Benefits

These vary according to the organization that directly pays the Coordinator. Some organizations do not cover benefits and many more do not cover benefits for employees who work below a certain number of hours. However, the average for benefits to a half-time Coordinator in Washington is approximately $3600 per year. This includes health insurance.

Office and Operating Supplies

A program serving approximately 35 individuals per month will be likely to spend about $1,500 per year on office and operating supplies, such as paper, pens, pencils, folders and staplers. This may include one copy each of some very basic texts, such as a dictionary and a thesaurus, and perhaps a video or two.

Telephone

When service already exists in the location, the cost of telephone service may be approximately $2,000 per year, including minimal long-distance calls and the charge rates of the local telephone service.

Travel

Although payment to employees of travel costs is a policy decision usually made before a SEd program begins, allowable purposes and amounts of monetary reimbursements for travel can significantly vary from program to program. We advise that a Supported Education budget include at least $1,000 for this if reach-out, recruitment, meetings, presentations and/or training will take the Coordinator (or other staff) away from the primary SEd Program site.

Other Expenses

Planners should also consider; equipment, professional services, training, advertising, rentals, insurance, public utilities, repairs and maintenance, and miscellaneous.

Textbooks for students or printing costs of handouts may be covered and can be included under the miscellaneous category or may be a specific line item in the budget. While these are potential expenses, and there may be more, these really depend on the program plan, circumstances, in-kind contributions from the site organization, possible other targeted revenues available, and choices of those involved. Programs must also include costs of having volunteers, if there are to be volunteers, such as for Labor and Industries Insurance coverage. Equipment should always include a computer, web access and telephone for the Coordinator. These are often in-kind contributions from the site organization, as may be some clerical assistance, parking, computer lab access and copying.

Program Implementation Task List

In the beginning of a new SEd program, it can be helpful for the coordinator(s) to know ahead of time what tasks will need to be completed. The structure of a tasks list may an important accommodation for coordinators and other staff who have psychiatric disabilities, in particular, but will be helpful to anyone starting a new SEd program. The following list covers the first three to four weeks, but it is not exhaustive and will need to be tailored to the particular circumstances of the program. Some of the tasks listed here will be ongoing.

Coordinator Tasks List—First Two Weeks

The tasks marked with an asterisk will be ongoing responsibilities, so schedule time for these.

- Meet with Human Resources staff to begin a personnel file and complete the W-2 form. Become familiar with facility policies and procedures, especially as they apply to the new SEd program. Attend the college's orientation if they offer one;

- Introduce self to co-workers, as soon as possible and appropriate;

- Schedule standing meeting times and any other trainings and orientations in your schedule book;

- Develop flyers and brochures for the program to send to college, mental health agency personnel and other agencies serving people with psychiatric disabilities, such as the Division of Vocational Rehabilitation (DVR), WorkSource, Social Security Administration (SSI and SSDI or SSA case workers) and the governmental or other entity funding the program. Include when Supported Education services will begin, an initial schedule and how to reach you.

- Put a sign on your door with your name, explanation of Supported Education, your hours and phone number. Get business cards;

- Make appointments with the college's Disabilities Office and Deans or division heads that oversee Adult Basic Education, Continuing Education, Counseling, Advising, and other appropriate departments to explain Supported Education and develop relationships. Explain how students may access Supported Education. Leave literature;*

- Set up your office, files, materials, and classroom space, as needed;

- Continue advertising for Supported Education participants by speaking about it at mental health facilities, advocacy association meetings and other appropriate gatherings. Call or see case managers. Contact local DVR offices;*

- Make sure the intake and assessment forms and processes are developed;

- Set class schedules;

- Meet with each person interested in Supported Education on a one-to-one basis as soon as possible after first contact;*

- Prepare lesson plans and curricula. Have handouts and teaching materials at least one week in advance of the class. Have lesson plans and schedule set for at least one month;

- Brief your supervisor at least once per week on your activities and progress. Seek help as needed. Write a descriptive memo of Supported Education plans and progress, and then distribute it to those who need to know and those who may be interested;*

- Contact the local literacy association or service, or the college's tutoring center, to work with SEd students, as needed. Contact the college foundation and other resources for free or low cost books and materials for students;*

- Conduct telephone outreach to SEd students weekly;*

- Continue to make Supported Education presentations to consumer groups, mental health centers, college personnel, advocacy groups, other services working with consumers and interested community members;*

- Complete forms for initial data collection and other purposes, as you begin work on the program goals and measurable objectives;

- Plan the advisory group, contact potential members and schedule the first meeting for near the end of the first quarter, if not before then;*

- Check with the supervisor and the contract on possible direction for completing program goals and measurable objectives, then on data needed and formats for data collection and reporting.*

CHAPTER 3
RIGHTS, POLICIES, PROCEDURES AND RELATED MATERIALS

Student Rights and Responsibilities

All students of the Supported Education Program have certain rights and responsibilities pertaining to participation in the program and college courses. Exercising these rights and responsibilities will better enable students to meet their educational goals while maintaining their status as students. Students who violate any of the responsibilities can expect program or college action to either correct the problem, or delay or terminate the student's participation, according to college policies and procedures concerning student discipline.

Student Rights

- To be treated fairly and with dignity;
- To not be discriminated against on the basis of disability, ethnicity, religion, gender, sexual orientation, marital status, national origin, citizenship, political affiliation, or age;
- To not be subject to sexual harassment;

- To state a complaint and file a grievance (See Grievance Policy and Procedures);

- To request and receive individualized assistance on tasks related to testing, registration, classroom accommodations, accessing funding and other resources for education and Supported Education course completion, as are possible within the scope of the Supported Education Program;

- To be given feedback concerning course assignments;

- To be provided reasonable accommodations related to a disability, as the student requests, and according to the guidelines stated in the Americans with Disabilities Act (ADA) and the provisions of the Supported Education Disability Accommodations Policy and Procedures;

- To be given access to all of the Policies, Procedures and other materials in the Supported Education Manual;

- To terminate from the Supported Education Program whenever she or he chooses, preferably by giving a reason to the Coordinator for that decision;

- To choose to return to the Program at a later date, unless deemed in imminent danger to self or others or highly disruptive in the classroom;

- To not have Program participation restricted or disallowed on any other grounds;

- To proceed from course to course, as possible within the Program's stated design, at one's own pace;

- To be referred by the Coordinator for additional assistance to any service that would enable the student to better meet his or her educational goals.

Student Responsibilities

- To respect the time constraints and capacities of the Coordinator and other Supported Education staff to help the student meet her or his educational goals;

- To not use, or have in possession, any illegal substance, alcohol or weapon while participating in the Program;

- To not use offensive language, engage in sexual harassment, or make racially or sexually derogatory remarks or create a hostile atmosphere through remarks or actions;

- To dress according to College campus standards for any Supported Education courses or otherwise while on the College campus;

- To not cheat, act aggressively towards staff or other students, steal or knowingly give false information to any Supported Education or College staff;

- To not smoke within any campus or Supported Education building;

- To respect the right of the Coordinator or other staff to maintain classroom focus and order;

- To respect the Coordinator's decisions concerning inclusion of visitors to classes and other functions;

- To respect the rights of Supported Education and other campus employees, and other students;

- To maintain other students' confidentiality by not divulging names or information to others;

- To read, or be read, and follow all procedures contained in the Program's Manual and College Campus rules as outlined in the College's Student Handbook (particularly concerning disability accommodations);

- To turn off pagers, cell phones or any other electronic devices that make noise in classes and groups;

- To listen, take notes as required, and follow through on all assignments and tasks by stated deadlines, unless accommodations for a disability are arranged with the Coordinator that exempt the student from such participation or extend deadlines;

- To ask questions, as needed, to understand the materials given and information conveyed.

Ethics

Purpose

To ensure the highest standard of ethical behavior in our supported education work with people who have psychiatric disabilities, the employing institution, co-workers, volunteers and colleagues in the education, rehabilitation and mental health fields, and to encourage professional growth that can improve the Program.

Definitions

Ethics—code of right and wrong; moral practices; conscientious, competent, noble and honest practices

Policy

It is the Policy of the Supported Education Program that the Coordinator and any other Program employees and volunteers shall abide by morally sound rules of conduct, including professionalism and commitment to professional growth. Lack of knowledge of such guidelines shall not be considered defense against any charge of unethical behavior. The policies and procedures of the employing institution, the policy and procedures herein and relevant laws shall be applied to any charge, due process and disciplinary action concerning unethical conduct.

Procedures

Conduct shall be:

- Legal;
- Respectful;
- Fair,
- Honest;
- Courteous;

- Focused on education of students, according to their individual needs, capacities, learning styles and preferences;

- Aware and careful of the risks of dual relationships with students, avoiding them when possible; and;

- Collaborative with others serving the student and with all persons connected to the Program.

Conduct shall not, in any way, compromise working relationships with students or others connected with the Program. This means that the Coordinator, staff and volunteers shall not, as examples:

- Engage in any monetary or service exchange, or seek to gain unfair advantage, with students, other staff or volunteers that is unauthorized by the Supervisor or for personal gain;

- Participate in, suggest, infer, or make jokes about any type of sexual behavior, on or off the job, with students;

- Compromise the reputation of any colleague in the field by discussing information or personal opinions about a colleague with students or in public;

- Divulge any information about a student, or allow access to records by other individuals, other than by the process and circumstances described in the Program's Confidentiality Policies and Procedures, relevant Mental Health Administrative Codes and Revised Codes of the state, and individual students' Releases of Information;

- Engage in, or allow, in the Program environment, discriminatory behavior, jokes, written material or display of such, or inference toward any student, colleague or other person or group on the basis of disability, ethnicity, religion, gender, sexual orientation or social class.

Professionalism and professional growth shall include, but not be limited to:

- Adhering to the employer's policies and procedures;

- Continually seeking and participating in continued learning, as possible;

- Evaluating the Program and attending to corrective actions indicated by such evaluation;

- Following best practice indications in the operations of the Program;
- Considering and implementing reasonable suggestions for change that could enhance the Program or further benefit students;
- Participating in professional groups and activities that can strengthen collegial relationships or advocacy efforts for students or potential students;
- Abiding by agreements with students and colleagues;
- Grading student work according to sound evaluation practices;
- Following all Program policies and procedures; and
- Encouraging, and supporting as possible, the professional development of students, former students, staff and volunteers.

Intake and Assessment

Purpose

The purpose of intake and assessment is to provide Supported Education (SEd) staff with information about the potential student, with the goals to; clarify SEd Program opportunities; discover student needs, expectations and plans; and identify coordinator recommendations.

Procedures

The intake is a source of initial information from which the potential student and coordinator plan and develop individual educational supports and resources.

The intake process may include, but shall not be limited to, an oral interview, a written questionnaire, a coordinator disclosure statement, and a confidentiality form.

The intake shall occur through a face-to-face, individual interview with the potential student. Information about past education, vocational interests, mental health supports, financial aid needs, initial goals, and expectations shall be part of the interview and shall be recorded on the intake form.

Ongoing assessment by the coordinator is shared with the student, based on the student's performance and attendance, and may be shared with the student's primary mental health service person if the student is in agreement with this and has signed a release of information.

✧ ✧ ✧ ✧

Intake Assessment Form

Name of Student: ______________________________

Quarter/Year: ______________________________

Student Address: ______________________________

Student Phone Number: ______________________________

____

Mental Health Clinic and Case Manager: ______________________________

____

What was your last completed year in school? ______________

What subjects were you best at? ______________________

____

What subjects were most difficult? ______________________

____

How would you describe your previous school experience?

____

Were you in any special programs that you are aware of?

____

Do you have a GED or high school diploma (which)?

____

What career goals do you have? What work interests you?

____

What, if any, educational goals do you have at this time?

____

Do you need financial assistance in order to continue your education?

____

In what ways can Supported Education assist you that you are aware of?

____

Have you taken a consumer/family class regarding mental illness and treatment?

____

Do you have a plan for managing symptoms of your psychiatric disorder?

____

I am interested in the following:

- ☐ One-to-one help with financial aid
- ☐ Supported Education preparatory classes
- ☐ Obtaining my GED or high school diploma
- ☐ Improving my reading, math, or writing level
- ☐ Help deciding my future educational goals
- ☐ Help deciding my future work goals
- ☐ Enrolling in college credit classes

Staff Signature ______________________________

Date ________________________

Disability Accommodations

Purpose

To ensure that any person applying to, or participating in, the Supported Education Program is aware of the right to reasonable accommodation related to a disability, according to the Americans with Disabilities Act (ADA), and that such accommodations are provided.

Definitions

See the Americans with Disabilities Act (ADA), which includes a definition of reasonable accommodation. See also the College policy and College Disabilities Office's procedures.

Policy

The Coordinator of the Supported Education Program shall ensure that each applicant and student is aware of the right to reasonable accommodation under the ADA for a disability. She or he shall also implement the proper accommodations for any meetings, class work and homework, and inform students of how to request accommodations on the job and in further education or training programs.

Procedures

- The Coordinator shall mail or give, in person, a written letter to the applicant concerning who to contact at the College's Disabilities Office by telephone or in person, the telephone number, building and office number. The instruction letter shall; explain that accommodations provided must be related to a disability and the potential for success in the Supported Education Program; reference the ADA; and explain that documentation from a physician or other disabilities professional must be provided before or at the time of the meeting with the Disabilities Specialist. Any applicant who the Coordinator believes may have difficulty with this process shall be provided assistance or the coordinator may refer the applicant to the appropriate assistance for completion of this process;

- The Coordinator shall also refer any student to the College's Disability Office for an accommodations assessment with the above instructions and assistance, if the student reports or appears to have difficulties related to a disability at any time during the student's Program participation;

- The Coordinator shall consult with the Disabilities Specialist whenever unsure whether a student's difficulties are related to a disability and refer to DVR, the case manager, therapist, physician, or other disabilities specialist for diagnosis and assessment of functioning, depending on what resource is indicated for the suspected or evident disability. Then, referral to the College's Disabilities Specialist for accommodations assessment shall be made;

- Whenever a student is enrolled as a DVR participant, the Coordinator, or case manager at the initiation of the Coordinator, or the student, shall contact DVR to request funding and provision of accommodations that have been found to be needed and above the cost limit that can be covered by the College. In the event that DVR is not able to serve the student, the coordinator shall seek other resources;

- The Coordinator, and anyone working under the direction of the Coordinator, shall follow the accommodations instructions of the College's Disabilities Office. They shall also implement any other reasonable accommodations for an applicant's or student's psychiatric disability that is found to be helpful to the student in his or her efforts to complete Program-related tasks;

- The Coordinator shall be responsible for ensuring that any other resources for accommodations are contacted, as needed. These may include; the Library for the Blind, state DSHS, a Developmental Disabilities Division, a university rehabilitation department., Easter Seals, or other resources.

Confidentiality

Purpose

To protect the confidentiality of each student and potential student concerning status as a mental health services recipient, progress in the Supported Education Program and performance in any college courses.

Policy

The Supported Education Program will ensure that program staff protect the confidentiality of students and potential students of the program.

Procedures

- The program will not disclose confidential information, including the fact a person is or has been a recipient of mental health services, sought information on SEd, or is or was a student, except with the informed and written consent of the; person interested in entering SEd, student or legally responsible guardian; or as described by statute, regulations and administrative codes of the state and federal governments;

- Release and/or exchange of information forms which include name, date, name and address of the program, name and address of the person or entity to whom the information is being provided, purpose of disclosure, specific kind of information to be disclosed, time frame according to state law, signature of the student, applicant or guardian and signature of a witness shall be included for releases and/or exchanges of student, or potential student seeking entry to SEd, information;

- Exceptions are specified by administrative codes and revised codes of the state;

- A copy of any disclosures requested and made, initiated by the Program or another entity to the Program, must be kept in the potential student's file. A revocation may be requested at any time in writing and the notice will be filed in the potential student's record with the release which has been revoked, unless disclosure is required by substantial action that has been taken in reliance on an authorization under law;

- Releases shall be fully dated, month, day and year, written in pen and no erasures or ink covering substances shall be used on the form;

- Personal demographics, program applications and any psychiatric intervention notes will be stored in a locked file and/or located in a locked room, accessible only to authorized program personnel.

✧ ✧ ✧ ✧

Consent for Release or Exchange of Information

The information to be disclosed is from records whose confidentiality is protected by state law. The law prohibits the recipient from making any further disclosure of this information without the specific written consent of the person to whom it pertains, or as otherwise permitted by state law. A general authorization for the release of medical or other information is not sufficient for this purpose. *Please complete in full and in pen.*

Student or Applicant Name: ______________________________

Date: ____

Is this for: *Release*? Yes ___ No ___ *Exchange*? Yes ___ No ___

Name and address of the entity to whom the information may be released:

____

Name and address of the entities between whom the information may be exchanged:

____

Purpose: *To support the academic success and safety of this student.*

Specific kind of information: *Only information that pertains to either my academic success or the safety of myself or others may be released or exchanged.*

This Release will expire upon the following dates or under the following conditions or events, unless the student chooses to revoke the consent in writing at an earlier date (no longer than time allowed by law).

I authorize the release or exchange of information as outlined above.

______________________________ ______________

Signature of Applicant or Student Date

______________________________ ______________

Signature of Witness (not program staff) Date

Program Evaluation

Purpose

The Partnership's recommended Program Evaluation methods have several purposes; accountability, focus, basis for program improvement and to judge effort, effectiveness and efficiency. Program evaluation helps to account for staff time spent and paid for, thus accounting to funders and administrators. It aids program staff and those connected to the program to focus on the program's purposes. It yields information on whether program objectives and goals are met, thereby providing a basis for continuance of, or need to revise, methods to reach the objectives and goals. It may even raise the question, and give direction for, changing goals and objectives.

Policy: It is the policy of Supported Education (SEd) to evaluate its effectiveness and effort on an ongoing basis and respond to the evaluation trends with decisions to remedy problematic operational methods to reach the program objectives and goals. Efficiency shall be measured as part of the budget monitoring function

Procedures

- The SEd Coordinator shall write the goals and objectives of the program with the input and authorization of the Supervisor. The Coordinator shall present these to the Advisory Board for review and consider their input concerning revisions;

- Goals may be altered no more than once per year and objectives, no more than quarterly and always in light of the program's funding contract, mission, description, and policies and procedures. Objectives should be both reasonable for the particular program and based on progress towards state-of-the art outcomes;

- While goals may be broad, somewhat nebulous and/or long-range, objectives shall be directly related to the goal — specific, measurable, achievable, reasonable and time-framed (SMART). Goals and/or objectives must reflect, but not be limited to, funding contract expectations;

- Measures shall be applied to each objective on a quarterly basis and documented in the Quarterly Program Evaluation Report;

- Measurement shall include, at the very least, per quarter:

    - Students in Supported Education program per class;
    - Intakes and assessments;
    - Students working while attending SEd Students in support groups;
    - Individual contacts with students and number of students served individually;
    - Phone contacts with students;
    - Students who have completed SEd courses;
    - Students in vocational training courses Students in GED classes;
    - Students in Adult Basic Education courses;
    - Students in college-level courses;
    - Students terminated from SEd courses before completion;
    - Returned students ;
    - Students completing their non-SEd courses;
    - Non-duplicated students served;
    - Or percentage student attendance in SEd.
    - Percent of student satisfaction;
    - Students graduated and from what types of educational programs and degrees;
    - Students who became employed following SEd, both having completed and not;
    - having completed SEd and non-SEd courses;
    - Presentations made by staff (can be per staff person);

  - SEd Student grades and the courses they take may also be of interest.

- The Quarterly Program Evaluation Report shall include narrative concerning the reasons for any discrepancies between objectives and measured outcomes and corrective actions planned. The Report shall then be presented for review to the Supervisor and Advisory Board on a quarterly basis for review. Advised revisions to methods or objectives shall be considered and made as soon as possible before the next Quarterly Program Evaluation Report. An objective should be revised if it, over the course of the quarter and not in the contract; a) is no longer deemed a meaningful step towards reaching program goals, b) measurement of it takes significant time from the Coordinator's other duties, or c) it does not meet the requirements and intentions of the mission, program description, contract, policies and procedures. These Reports, or any parts of them, shall not be used for marketing or any other form of public disclosure.

- A composite Annual Program Evaluation Report shall reflect each quarter of the year and be presented to the Supervisor, Advisory Board, and funding Contractor within the first month of each new fiscal year. This Annual Report, or any parts of it, shall not reveal the identities of program students and applicants, including any student demographics. Otherwise, the Program Evaluation Report shall be authorized by the State's Human Subjects Research Review Board before release to any but government funders of the program and paid staff.

Program Evaluation Reports may take the place of, or be the larger part of, outcomes reports designed by a funding contractor if the contractor agrees, keeping in mind the contract's requirement for submission. Format may also be determined by the contracting entity. Some funders will require, or even provide, a software program for this purpose.

The Process of Program Evaluation

Probably the most difficult parts of program evaluation are the beginning and end, writing the goals and measurable objectives, gathering the data on a daily basis and deciding what the quarterly and annual outcomes mean for the program. Once the goals and measurable objectives are written, systems and the habit of data collection on a daily basis can be challenging. Then, when established, the data collection can become just another routine, like unlocking the door, turning on the lights and checking for voice and email messages.

Some suggestions for good data collection are: integrate it into other routine activities, where possible (such as keeping attendance in each class, while saying good morning to students); keep it simple (check marks and numbers will likely be enough if you've really made the program objectives measurable); establish certain daily times you gather data (during and as part of individual assessments, as part of each class and group, at the mid-point and end of each day, as examples); keep all daily statistics forms readily available for your use and accessible for monthly and quarterly composites. Mark the days of each month and quarter for these tasks on your calendar for a year at a time.

✧ ✧ ✧ ✧

Figure 3:1. Illustration of Steps from Data Gathering through Report Writing

Step 1

Collect Data Daily

Step 2

Enter to Statistics Form Monthly

Step 3

Create Quarterly Program Evaluation Reports

Step 4

Create Annual Program Evaluation Report

Chapter 4

Personnel

Supported Education staff must be able to perform and balance a number of responsibilities in the arena of human services and education, in addition to practicing more basic habits and skills necessary to employment. The attributes and capacities of the person, as necessary to perform the responsibilities of the position, should be considered perhaps as much or even more than higher level skills for the job. In addition, if the Coordinator has a psychiatric disability, certain preparation for providing accommodations also needs to be considered in hiring. The person selected may need to use time off for attention to mental health needs. Consequently, the program should provide a back-up staff person, work-study student or intern in case of absence of the Coordinator so that disruption to students is avoided. Inclusion of an Assistant Coordinator on staff, even for just a few hours per week, has other advantages as well. The roles or responsibilities of Supported Education Assistant, Coordinator, Supervisor and the Advisory Board are described here, as is the ideal composition of the Advisory Board.

Basic Habits and Skills to Consider in Hiring

The following are some of the most agreed-upon skills and habits that are basic to most jobs: To check on these when hiring is commonplace.

- Punctuality;
- Respect for others;
- Written and verbal competence;
- Completion of tasks by deadlines;
- Organization;
- Following of directions;
- Constructive acceptance of feedback and supervision;
- Regular attendance;
- Attention to established rules.

Attributes and Capacities of Supported Education Personnel

Some of the important personal attributes and capacities for success and effectiveness in Supported Education direct service roles follow:

- Warmth, interest and listening are essential to forming positive helping relationships;

- Good organization and communication are necessary to managing day-to-day operations of a program;

- Respect for diversity, an active learning orientation and good listening are important for conveying information to a diverse group of individuals;

- A sense of fairness, creativity and flexibility, with a willingness to direct classroom order, are required to balance the needs of individuals with those of the group;

- Being an active learner is essential to providing current information, referrals and understanding the diverse challenges and needs of students;

- Separating personal issues from work is critical because these can divert from the work at hand and result in confusion and boundary issues for students;

- Initiating work tasks is important because Supported Education is not rote labor: No supervisor will remain on site, no pre-arranged task list and no fixed routine can guide SEd staff through all of the various tasks of every work day;

- Maintaining healthy role boundaries with students is necessary, and should be limited to, focus on meeting students' learning needs;

- Keeping accurate records requires attention to detail in establishment of routine methods for data collection and to meeting regular deadlines for data collection;

- Managing stressful situations in ways that don't disrupt the program necessitates the process of recognizing stress in oneself, proactive planning for handling stress and practicing use of any number of positive, personal coping mechanisms;

- Prioritizing tasks according to student needs and program structures is often essential to effectiveness in Supported Education program;

- Working as a team member with advisory board members, supervisor, work-study personnel and interns;

The Roles of the Supported Education Assistant

There are several ways to ensure back-up for the Coordinator in case of absence. Hiring a part-time Assistant can fill this need. An Assistant can also broaden the program's capacity for serving additional or hard-to-reach students, offering more in-depth services, and bring additional skills and attributes to the program. Assistants can be assigned some of the tasks more suited to that person than the person in the Coordinator position, often tasks that are aligned with the special talents and interests of the person or responsibilities that don't especially need the hands-on attention of the Coordinator.

Students on work-study have been employed in these positions in Washington State, but because of the quarterly nature of work study, this can be a patchwork and frustrating solution to meet ongoing and unexpected program needs and requirements for particular skills. Instead, a regularly employed assistant, working a set schedule with a particular set of duties and some functional overlap with the Coordinator, for cross-training purposes, is a better solution. While the Assistant may work far fewer hours per week, back-up and extension of program capacities are attained. Otherwise, the supervisor may be needed to provide this. In any case, the supervisor will probably still be needed for assistance, but with an assistant hired, this should be only from time to time.

Supported Education Coordinator Job Description

The Supported Education Coordinator's job is to coordinate, promote, develop and implement supported education for clients of mental health services within the mental health catchment area. Responsibilities include, but are not limited to the following:

- Provide educational intake and counseling to applicants, using an individualized and tailored approach;
- Market and recruit for the program;
- Teach or assist in teaching preparatory classes;
- Serve as an advocate for students to solve issues concerning their education;
- Inform and guide students into college course work;
- Provide support to students in class; inform and refer students to tutoring services as they are available;
- Facilitate and market educational support group;
- Prepare attendance, progress and outcome reports;
- Provide technical assistance to college staff on ADA;
- Conduct advisory board meetings and provide data of quarterly program statistics as needed;
- Develop and/or adapt curricula for Supported Education program preparatory classes;
- Meet with supervisor to report progress on a regular basis.

The Roles of Supported Education Supervisor

The supervisor of the Supported Education Program and Program staff shall:

- Assist the coordinator/staff in developing employment accommodations as needed;

- Develop a close working relationship that allows Supported Education coordinator/staff to readily feel supported; and freely exchange problems, issues and concerns;

- Allow flexibility in coordinator work schedule as an accommodation;

- If appropriate, be available to act as liaison and support system in cross systems meetings and substitute for coordinator if needed;

- Conduct program development tasks and monitor completion on a regular and continuing basis;

- Contact designated and appropriate people in the field for technical assistance when needed;

- Actively advocate for the Supported Education coordinator/staff, persons with mental illness and the Supported Education Program;

- Oversee the budget.

Supported Education Advisory Board Member Roles

The Advisory Board's role is to assist in the planning, development and implementation of a quality Supported Education program. Advisory Board members represent a high level of expertise, as well as information links to other agencies within the community.

The purpose of the Supported Education Advisory Board is to:

- Review Supported Education curricula;
- Assist in program evaluation;
- Interpret the program to the community (agencies, businesses and individuals);
- Work to develop partnerships with the Supported Education program in the community;
- Recommend additions, modifications or deletions to the existing program.

Membership of Supported Education Advisory Board

The Supported Education Advisory Board members will be representative of those disciplines, public agencies, departments or organizations with which consumers of mental health services are most closely affiliated (such as Departments of Vocational Rehabilitation, vocational services in mental health agencies and college disabilities offices). Members will be drawn from the mental health facilities locally, will be those by the nature of their work and/or perspective who have some knowledge of the population who will be served and will be a diverse group of individuals, including consumers and family members.

CHAPTER 5

MARKETING AND FORMING ALLIANCES

Marketing of Supported Education and forming the necessary supportive alliances are highly dependent on how the mental health system is organized, its size, nature and the environment. Marketing is the word we'll use here to encompass advertising to potential students and mental health service providers, and to the formation of relationships with others who can be supportive in one way or another. It is clear in the section on developing a program that initial alliances are formed in the early stages of planning, but work on this must continue. Although the following are not exhaustive lists, some of the key sectors and their constituents are listed in this Section.

Posters, brochures and mail-outs can be used for marketing, but system-wide newsletters and email lists through administrative entities in the system can often also be used. Marketing can also occur through agency newsletters, college newspapers, web sites and links on related topic Internet sites. It is not enough, though, to advertise and assume that all or most people who have psychiatric disabilities in the community will become aware of, or be willing to try, Supported Education.

Regular, personal visits by the Coordinator or other staff, if there are others, to mental health centers to talk with potential students and service providers helps ongoing awareness and decreases anxieties or misperceptions that people may have about the program. Becoming a familiar, friendly face is critical to convincing potential students, in particular, to give the program a try. Some coordinators even complete intakes and assessments at the centers they visit and offer some of the initial classes and individual assistance meetings there.

Students may usually be people served in the publicly funded mental health system. However, many other programs and places might also be considered in getting the word out to potential students. Some college students have psychiatric disabilities and will welcome assistance to remain and succeed in college. Some communities have programs or places where people who have psychiatric disabilities participate or receive services other than mental health services. Some people in hospitals are able to take advantage of educational opportunities. Supported Education can be part of an excellent transition to the community from the hospital, but some people will remain in the hospital setting while still accomplishing something important through Supported Education.

Community-Wide

Here are some possible places to advertise:

- Consumer groups;
- Food banks;
- Department of Social And Health Services offices;
- Division of Vocational Rehabilitation offices;
- Colleges;
- Hospital psychiatric units;
- Community health clinics;
- Senior citizens' centers;
- Shelters;
- Mental health centers;
- Private for-profit mental health service providers;
- Clothing banks;
- Crisis services programs;

- Community service centers;
- Low-cost housing programs.

Although titles differ from area to area, the idea in forming alliances is to be in touch with people who have resources, knowledge, skills, and contacts or can otherwise do something supportive for students or the program. Here are some of the service providers coordinators should contact. Some of these should become long-term alliances:

Alliances

College Site(s) or College(s) Affiliated with Program

- Registrar;
- Assessment center director;
- Adult basic education director;
- Disabilities specialist;
- Dean (or vice president) of student services;
- GED director;
- Learning center director;
- Director of financial aid.

Consumer-operated Programs or Consumer Associations

- Peer centers;
- Drop-in centers;
- Recovery groups;
- Psychoeducation groups;
- Consumer groups or associations;
- Consumer-operated agencies and businesses.

Mental Health Agencies

- Executive directors ;
- Clinical directors;
- Staff training directors;
- Vocational program managers;
- Case management program managers;
- Case managers;
- Clubhouse directors and staff;
- Psychosocial or psychiatric rehabilitation directors and staff.

Advocacy Groups

- Protection and advocacy services;
- Local National Alliance for the Mentally Ill chapters;
- Ombuds Services;

Hospitals

- Patient and family education departments;
- Administrators;
- Staff training departments;
- Social workers;
- Occupational therapists;
- Family groups;
- Nurses, doctors and other direct service providers;
- Rehabilitation departments;

Mental Health Professional Associations Local Chapters and Conferences

Some alliances will result in Advisory Board memberships, but most will be people willing to do something or give helpful information for a student, students or the program in the course of their work. The excitement and promise of Supported Education will prompt some people to go out of their way to assist, but some people may not be particularly inspired to help at all. They may come around later, but meanwhile, if there is another person in the same position to help, don't hesitate to ask. If there isn't, it may be time to do a little more in-depth education about why Supported Education is such an exciting prospect for many people with psychiatric disabilities.

While there may be an inherent element of reciprocity in some of these relationships, it is often possible to offer support to potential allies in their endeavors as well. Gratitude, thank you notes and recognition of help from specific people can also go a long way towards forming the alliances that are needed to develop and maintain effective Supported Education programs.

CHAPTER 6

PROGRAM CONTENT

Each Supported Education program develops individually and offers somewhat differing program components, yet courses designed to prepare or reacquaint the student to post secondary entrance are usually a part of the Supported Education program and fall into several categories.

Orientation/Readiness Course

This course is designed to acquaint the student with the college campus milieu; it offers an overview of rules, procedures, resources on campus, financial aid options, tutoring assistance and the college registration process.

Goal Setting/Career Planning Course

This course assists students to identify their personal strengths and weaknesses and their vocational areas of interest. Students are supported and guided as they develop educational and vocational goals and then develop steps to achieve these goals.

Study Skills Course

This course assists students in their understanding of ADA and appropriate accommodations. Students are taught the art of note taking, text reading, test taking, time management and use of college resources that will support these skills on an ongoing basis.

Educational Support Group

This group, rather than a formal class, allows natural supports to develop. Members of the support group identify and assist each other in overcoming barriers, such as stigma, while in the process of continuing one's post secondary education. Typically, each group has an identified topic that is discussed by participants at each meeting (symptom management, stress reduction methods, etc.).

Lesson Planning

The most critical reason for writing and following a lesson plan for each class is that these plans help the instructor to be prepared and stay on task in the classroom. This can be difficult when students have many questions and frequently want to contribute. Although students should be encouraged in this at times, it can create confusion for other students and the instructor may run out of time just trying to keep up with student queries and personal examples. Sometimes, it's necessary to ask students to see the instructor after the class or to hold questions and comments until a segment of the lesson is presented. Some students do best at handling the anxiety that often seems to prompt many questions and comments if they write down their questions for later.

Figure 6:1. Typical Lesson Plan Format

Lesson Plan

Course:

Lesson:

Goals:

Equipment & Materials:

Procedures & Activities:

Teacher Notes & Suggestions:

Supporting Materials:

College Supports

Most college campuses have a special needs office and/or coordinator who assists in the completion of disability documentation and identification of accommodations. Other resources that may assist Supported Education students are tutoring services, career counseling centers, computer labs and math/writing labs that offer tutoring and individualized resources in varied subject and content areas.

Tutoring for Adult Basic Education

Many Supported Education students need to improve basic skills (reading, writing and math) yet are interested and desirous of continuing their post secondary education. Many students were developing symptoms of their illness and missed significant areas of learning. Learning to manage their illness along with improved medications and resources make it valuable for the student to begin on those basic skills not adequately learned earlier and continue on with their education.

Adult basic education instruction is an integral feature of community colleges. Quality ABE (Adult Basic Education) and ESL (English as a Second Language) programs are designed to introduce a student to beginning levels of math, reading and writing through the level of high school completion. Students may find these tutoring programs a necessary method of attaining or regaining skills inherent in successful community living and the pursuance of any vocation or degree program. The Supported Education Coordinator can assist in accessing these valuable resources.

Reach Out/ Stop Out

Significant elements of Supported Education programs are the flexibility of the program and the ongoing duration of the program for students with changing needs. Many students interrupt the continued post secondary educational program for varied reasons, one of which may be the return or worsening of psychiatric symptoms. At these times, most Supported Education programs have a reach-out and stop-out plan enabling students to return to their education programs at a later time when re-stabilization has been achieved. Coordinators reach-out to assist the student in the process of setting up a time out from their educational responsibilities by problem-solving and interceding for them with issues such as incompletes and financial aid appeals. Stop-outs often occur when students feel unable to continue classes, but still want to continue towards their goals at a later time, when they are experiencing fewer stressors.

Teaching Strategies

While the Supported Education coordinator does not necessarily have to have strong teaching skills, it certainly is an advantage to have some natural skill for the process of teaching. There are, however, strategies to follow that can make the learning process more successful for both the Supported Education Coordinator as well as Supported Education students.

Teaching persons with mental illness can be a teaching challenge for numerous reasons.

Students have often lost much self-esteem as a result of the experience of, residual disabling effects of, and others' reactions to, their disorders. Fear of further failure can make progress in a classroom setting slow. If the consumer in the Supported Education classroom is still experiencing symptoms, learning new and/or challenging information can be arduous.

We also know that anxiety effects learning; Supported Education Coordinators need to find ways to assist in the learning process (e.g. relaxation exercises, sitting apart from the other students in a classroom, positive visualization). Managing a major illness and adjusting to life in a community setting, while moving to an identity of student rather than consumer, is a huge and daunting task. Fear of success, then, can be as challenging as that of failure. These need to be considered in the process of re-entry to post-secondary or remedial education.

Some teaching strategies follow:

- Ad Lib: Look for the teachable moment and be willing to stray from lecture style by using unplanned examples, dramatics or comedy that particularly fit the moment;

- Adapt: An instructor should revise methods and content to fit the needs of the students as it becomes apparent that the lesson, as planned, is not meeting the learning goal;

- Simplify: Instructors should be aware of the levels of complexity students can handle at the particular time and stick to emphasizing the most needed information. Too much detail can be distracting and may be extraneous to the learning goal;

- Incremental teaching: Complex or long pieces of information should be separated into bite-sized chunks. This can be done, as examples, through separating information into consecutive days, by stopping to review or discuss between increments and by giving students an opportunity to learn in a step by step process;

- Successive assignments and breaking down information into sub-topics;

- Experiential: Teach using varied modalities, such as scenarios, role-playing, problem-solving, real practice and demonstration;

- Repetition: Few students learn on the first try;

- Meaningful Curriculum: This means that the instructor must teach to what is, or soon will be, meaningful to the students in that particular class because they need, or will need, to use it;

- Rapport: Many students shut down when they don't feel a sense of rapport with the instructor. The instructor must balance warmth, empathy, sensitivity and recognition of individual students with relaying information and giving direction. Students learn best from role models with whom they can identify and rapport assists that identification;

- Consistency: Consistency in the class schedule and expectations of students is crucial. Some predictability in an instructor's approach, whether in presentation style, adherence to the lesson plan and interaction with students, helps students concentrate on the information too;

- Awareness of student deficits and strengths: Capitalize on strengths by using methods and dialogue that tie into experiences, attributes, skills and capacities of students;

- Appropriate curriculum: Courses must be geared to the common needs of the group for reaching their shared learning goals. In turn, the goal of the course must match a part, or even the whole, of the students' learning goals;

- Learning readiness—Students must be ready for the information presented: If they don't have the foundation first, they will not be able to build on it.

Many of the teaching strategies used in adult education classrooms for people with learning disabilities are successful with people returning to school while managing a psychiatric disability. These are very specific methods intended for persons who may want to learn, but are still experiencing some difficulty with the process of learning. There are numerous helpful and simple suggestions for teaching that are basic to most adult education literature. Some of these are:

- Develop a simple lesson plan for each class session. This acts as a blueprint or a guide for class as opposed to using a rigid script;

- Choose a physical setting that is quiet and free from distractions;

- Develop rapport with each student when possible;

- Involve participants;

- The learning and teaching materials need to apply to student goals;

- Presentations must be clear, sequential and easy to hear;
- The instructor is a facilitator of learning; students do not expect teachers to know all there is to know about a subject, but they do expect the teacher to facilitate their learning;
- Vary teaching activities;
- Allow for individual differences and styles of learning;
- Make sure students are aware of course requirements and teacher expectations.

Other suggested instructional strategies from the Division of Adult Education and Literacy are:

- Break down tasks into small increments of learning and present them to the student in a paced manner;
- Present a variety of short assignments;
- Make sure the student has acquired one skill before presenting the next skill in the sequence of learning tasks;
- Structure assignments for the student and provide frequent feedback about the quality and appropriateness of work completed;
- Provide activities that allow the student to experience small successes in order to enhance his/her self-concept;
- Use as many modalities (sight, hearing, speaking and touch) as possible when presenting material. Making information available through different senses helps students to be active learners who use their strongest channels to get information;

- Capitalize on the student's strengths. For example, if the student is a good listener and can follow oral directions well, present materials orally. Teaching through the student's strengths helps to strengthen weak areas;

- Teach new concepts in as concrete a way as possible. It is often easier for students to learn the theory after its practical application;

- Relate new material to everyday life whenever possible. This can make abstract concepts more understandable;

- If possible, provide the student an opportunity to repeat verbally what has been taught as a check for accuracy: This can take place during the lesson or after class.

It is especially important to pay attention to self-concept enhancement when working with adults. Opportunities for student success should be maximized. Instructors should encourage students to obtain the help of the following assistive devices and methods, if needed:

- Note takers and/or readers;

- Tutors;

- Tape recorders for taping classroom instruction, preparing homework, and taking tests;

- Computers, calculators and other types of equipment suitable for classroom and homework;

- Audiocassettes for instruction and test taking;

- Recorded texts and voice indexing approaches;

- Other assistive devices and methods for helping students who have other disabilities in addition to psychiatric disabilities.

College Registration Process

The process of registering for credits can initially be complex and confusing. The role of Supported Education Coordinator includes assisting SEd students with this process. Some important registration information follows:

- See a registration advisor to select courses one placement testing and Supported Education preparation have been completed. This is most important for the student who has college credits already and is working towards a degree or certification. Advisors can assist with course selection, interpret results of college placement assessments, review transcripts and provide information to or from other colleges. At the onset of a student's return to post-secondary education, registering through the Disabilities Office is helpful. Staff in that office can conduct the registration process;

- Currently enrolled students are normally prioritized for registration;

- SEd preparation courses are non-credit and, in most cases, have no fee attached. This is generally the case for Adult Basic Education courses too. In both cases, the registration process is usually required;

- Many colleges have web sites at which registration can be completed;

- Registration advisors and other staff can assist late registration, changes in schedule and withdrawals, as well;

- Enrollment and financial need will determine if the student is a candidate for financial aid. The Financial Aid Office staff can assist with the application process. Continued financial aid is contingent on academic progress;

- Sometimes, grant makers and the financial aid office will agree to fund the student's part-time participation in college because of the disability, even though they rarely advertise this.

CHAPTER 7
STUDENT RESOURCES

Knowledge of resources and skills in accessing assistive devices and other accommodations are important for many students with disabilities. While Supported Education classes or workshops can provide the necessary information, not every SEd student will need or want to sit through long explanations of these. Much of this information is provided individually, as the need arises. The coordinator cannot be expected to be up-to-date and thoroughly informed on all of the resources either. This, again, is where relationships with colleagues on and off campus are very important.

When needed by the student, the coordinator, another staff person or even an experienced student should accompany the student to access information on campus, to ensure that the pertinent information is both provided to, and understood by, the student. Finding and arranging financial assistance is one of the most challenging and anxiety producing processes many people with psychiatric disabilities face in going back to school. SEd classes can include filling out financial aid applications and other paper work. This can be an efficient way to begin the process once the following information is provided.

PELL Grants

What is a Federal Pell Grant?

A Federal Pell Grant, unlike a loan, does not have to be repaid. Generally, Pell Grants are awarded only to undergraduate students who have not earned a bachelor's or professional degree. (A professional degree is typically earned after earning a bachelor's degree in a field such as medicine, law, or dentistry.) In some cases, you may receive a Pell Grant for attending a post-baccalaureate teacher certification program. For many students, Pell Grants provide a foundation of financial aid to which other aid may be added.

How do I qualify?

To determine if you're eligible financially, the U.S. Department of Education uses a standard formula, established by Congress, to evaluate the information you report when you apply. The formula produces an Expected Family Contribution (EFC) number. Your Student Aid Report (SAR) contains this number and will tell you if you're eligible.

How much money can I get?

Awards for the 2000-2001 award year (July 1, 2000 to June 30, 2001) will depend on program funding. The maximum award for the 1999-2000 award year was $3,125. You can receive only one Pell Grant in an award year. How much you get will depend not only on your EFC but also on your cost of attendance, whether you're a full-time or part-time student, and whether you attend school for a full academic year or less. You may not receive Pell Grant funds from more than one school at a time.

How will I be paid?

Your school can credit the Pell Grant funds to your school account, pay you directly (usually by check), or combine these methods. The school must tell you in writing how and when you'll be paid and how much your award will be. Schools must pay you at least once per term (semester, trimester, or quarter). Schools that do not use formally defined, traditional terms must pay you at least twice per academic year.

Can I Receive a Federal Pell Grant If I Am Enrolled less than Half Time?

Yes, if you're otherwise eligible. You won't receive as much as if you were enrolled full time, but your school must disburse your Pell Grant funds in accordance with your enrollment status and cannot refuse you an award simply because you're enrolled less than half time. (Dept. of Education, 2000)

Direct and FFEL Stafford Loans

Direct and FFEL Stafford Loans are the U.S. Education Department's major form of self-help aid. Direct Stafford Loans are available through the William D. Ford Federal Direct Loan (Direct Loan) Program and FFEL Stafford Loans are available through the Federal Family Education Loan (FFEL) Program; The terms and conditions of a Direct Stafford or a FFEL Stafford are similar. The major differences between the two are the source of the loan funds, some aspects of the application process, and the available repayment plans. Under the Direct Loan Program, the funds for your loan are lent to you directly by the U.S. government. Under the FFEL Program, the funds for your loan are lent to you from a bank, credit union, or other lender that participates in the FFEL Program. The Direct and FFEL programs also offer PLUS Loans for parents of dependent students and Consolidation Loans.

What kinds of Direct and FFEL Stafford Loans are available?

Direct and FFEL Stafford Loans are either subsidized or unsubsidized. You can receive a subsidized loan and an unsubsidized loan for the same enrollment period. A subsidized loan is awarded on the basis of financial need. You will not be charged any interest before you begin repayment or during authorized periods of deferment. The federal government "subsidizes" the interest during these periods. An unsubsidized loan is not awarded on the basis of need. You'll be charged interest from the time the loan is disbursed until it is paid in full. If you allow the interest to accumulate, it will be capitalized--that is, the interest will be added to the principal amount of your loan and additional interest will be based upon the higher amount.

Who Can Get a Direct or FFEL Stafford Loan?

If you're a regular student enrolled in an eligible program of study at least halftime, you may receive a Direct or FFEL Stafford Loan. You must also meet other general eligibility requirements. (Dept. of Education, 2000)

Division of Vocational Rehabilitation (DVR)

The Division of Vocational Rehabilitation (DVR or VR), a part of a state's Department of Social and Health Services, is familiar to many people with disabilities. DVR can assist people who have disabilities with the expenses of job training and with job placement, but the state, locale and even the individual DVR counselor have some latitude in how people are served. It is critical for Supported Education coordinators to form relationships with one or more DVR counselors. DVR can also be a source of referral to

SEd for potential students. Including a DVR counselor or two on the supported Education Advisory Board may be advantageous.

Some DVR Counselors are quite accustomed to providing funds for basic education or GED classes. Some will readily pay for vocational training courses, often the shorter in duration the more likely to be acceptable to VR. Others will support students working towards degrees. DVR can also provide skills training assistance for the purpose of upgrading specific job skills needed for advancement from an existing job.

It is important to remember in working with DVR that the student is likely to be viewed first and foremost, as a DVR participant who is planning on going to work or advancing in current work. The DVR Counselor will require documentation of the disability from the mental health service provider, may require the person to attend job search and preparation workshops, special assessments, basic education classes that may not be at the college and develop a plan with the Counselor.

Supported Education coordinators who understand local DVR agencies and refer to one or two familiar DVR counselors may be able to advocate best for students by both preparing students for the eligibility requirements for DVR and urging their DVR counselors to concentrate on providing SEd students with what the students have specifically stated are their training and job goals. If the student has not determined a job goal, the DVR Counselor may help the student with that, but usually, any training or related expenses paid by DVR will need to be directly related to a job goal on the student's VR plan.

Depending on the state, DVR offices may be either closely or loosely affiliated with WorkSource. What this means for a Supported Education student is that some WorkSource staff may question serving, or refer, a SEd student to DVR, and under some circumstances, DVR may refer a student on to other WorkSource programs.

Community Support: Regional, County and State Mental Health Flex Funds

In some states, flexible mental health dollars are available according to special, individual needs or priorities that have probably not been addressed by other budget allocation. Sometimes, these funds are simply earmarked for an array of needs of mental health consumers, although upon application or request, there will undoubtedly be some process for deciding who gets the funds and for what purposes. SEd coordinators should know if college tuition, books or related return-to-school expenses could be covered for SEd students.

Educational Opportunities and Resource Center Grants

The Supported Education program's college site should have information on Education Opportunities and Resource Center Grants, either in the disabilities office, the financial aid office or through the advising office. Otherwise, information can often be found on the State's Education Department web site. Grants for tuition and related expenses, for both individuals and groups, are usually listed.

Scholarships

Not all scholarships are based on the person's academic record. Many are based on need, field of study, affiliations and other factors. Information on scholarships can be found in a number of places. Start with the college where the Supported Education Program is located. College advisors can help sort through innumerable options. The Internet is also loaded with sites. Here are a few of the 29,000 or so on the web:

- www.finaid.com
- www.salliemae.com
- www.freschinfo.com

Researching scholarships and filling out the required forms can be very time-consuming. Supported Education coordinators may decide it is most efficient to refer students to a colleague on campus who helps students with this on a regular basis, sometimes advisors, sometimes disabilities specialists and sometimes staff in the student counseling center.

WorkSource/WorkForce Development

In Washington, WorkSource is a partnership of a state's Employment Security Department with Temporary Assistance to Needy Families, former Private Industry Councils (Job Training Partnership Act), now revised and called the Workforce Investment Act (WIA) programs, local offices of the Division of Vocational Rehabilitation (DVR) and sometimes other vocational programs. Not all states have implemented WorkSource at this writing. WorkForce Boards oversee WorkSource operations.

WIA funding can sometimes be used to help a student with the costs of school courses or training. In Washington, for instance, eligible (means tested) single people with disabilities can be counted as one-person families. People with disabilities who have family members living with them are eligible for increasing amounts of assistance, depending on the number of people in the family.

WorkSource Centers provide all the information, technology and services business needs to thrive and job seekers need to achieve successful careers. They represent a unique concept in the labor market—everything in one place. WorkSource Center Services are delivered to customers in a variety of ways, including: self-directed efforts, such as kiosks or via the Internet Group programs and activities, such as workshops; one-on-one consultations; and training programs and business consultations. The backbone of Washington's system is a set of 12 WorkSource Centers located in Bellingham, North Seattle, Renton, Shelton, Omak, Spokane, Walla Walla, White Salmon, Bellevue, Cowlitz/Wahkiakum, and two in Vancouver. WorkSource Centers will open within the next few years throughout the country. (State of WA, 2000)

In Washington, as an example, affiliate sites that serve special populations, will also be electronically linked to the system and self-service stations, called WorkSource Connections, will be offered at all Centers, Affiliates and other public and private organizations for customers needing less assistance. Services for job seekers include:

- Free use of computers, copiers, phones, faxes and other career resources;
- Internet access to jobs;
- Job referral and placement;
- Classes on how to get and keep a job;
- Information on the fastest growing jobs and wages;
- Referral to training and other community services;
- Access to Unemployment Insurance;
- Translation services.

WorkSource is a joint venture of organizations dedicated to addressing Washington State's employment needs, including:

- Business;
- Labor;
- Employment Security Department;
- Community and Technical Colleges;
- Department of Social and Health Services;
- Workforce Training and Education Coordinating Board;
- Superintendent of Public Instruction;
- The Governor's Office;

- Partners at the local level include state partner agencies, as well as non-profits and local government agencies. (State of WA, 2000).

WIA (Workforce Invest Act) programs can provide funds for one or more person families, especially suitable for people who have psychiatric disabilities living below the poverty line are available through WorkSource or outsourced agencies for people who meet their area's WIA eligibility criteria. Many offices use WIA funds to support people in educational and training programs by paying for tuition, books, back-to-school expenses, transportation and other needs while attending classes, but not all use WIA funds for anything other than directly for employment assistance. However, rules and processes vary from state to state, and even within states, among WIA programs.

In Washington state, public colleges and universities are automatically WorkSource Partners and, since Supported Education is usually located at a college or university, no vendorship or partnership application is needed from the Supported Education program or the larger educational institution housing it if a student from Supported Education is applying for assistance to attend that school or another college or university. A WorkSource office with a WIA program may be located on campus. In this case, it is wise for the SEd coordinator to become especially familiar with their personnel, eligibility criteria and processes, and share with them what the Supported Education program does. This introduction may ease access for SEd students later.

It is important to have a clear understanding of what the WIA program, whether located at WorkSource or in another agency, can offer before sending a Supported Education student to them. Supported Education staff may need to call with the student to make a first appointment, or the student may be required to attend a regularly scheduled, open orientation first. It is important to understand that SEd students must be clear with WIA staff about what they are seeking, the costs and how it relates to an employment goal, so SEd staff should advise students they refer of this beforehand.

Some students may need the coordinator's, or other SEd staff person's, in-person help during the first one or two WIA meetings. It is important for the case manager or another mental health service person to advocate for the student with WIA, sometimes even participate in admissions decision-making meetings with WIA program staff within a day or two after the student has attended an orientation. The Coordinator should suggest this to the mental health provider, who may not be aware of the need for this. Applicants are not usually allowed to attend these meetings.

In any case, coordinators themselves should learn the eligibility criteria, what documents and information a prospective applicant should bring to the orientation meeting, what the local WIA program will cover for an eligible person and experience the entire process themselves, to the degree possible, at least once with a student to become familiar with it. Coordinators will likely need the information later for other students.

College Foundation and Other Foundation Grants

The college campus student counseling, advising or career center will have information on these grants, if and when they are available. Campus newsletters often include notice of such grants.

Tuition Waivers

Many colleges will waive tuition for certain students under certain circumstances. Again, check with the financial aid, disabilities or advising offices. Make sure that SEd students who are granted these, understand exactly what they cover and for how many quarters.

WorkFirst
Temporary Assistance for Needy Families (TANF)
Recipients and TANF Eligible

WorkFirst programs may help a parent or parents go back to school. In most states, TANF is means-dependent: Eligibility is determined on the basis of income below a certain point, depending on the state, and on being a parent. Services differ from state to state, but some offer the following or more. WorkFirst participants and other low-income working parents may be eligible for the following services:

- Educational planning;

- Financial assistance for tuition, fees, and books for short-term vocational and basic skills training for wage and skill progression;

- Pre-employment training that is customized to meet an individual employer's or group of employers' needs;

- Individualized or small group pre-employment training that may use existing classes;

- WorkFirst/Work Study that combines the work and learning components of a WorkFirst participant's activities;

- Referral to Working Connections Childcare for funding assistance while a WorkFirst or other low-income working parent is in class or studying; and Payment of GED testing fee.

Find WorkFirst by using the telephone directory, asking a college (there may be a program on the campus where Supported Education is located) or calling WorkSource. Supervisors of

Supported Education coordinators can often be very helpful in locating such campus and community resources for sponsorship of education or training.

In some states, WorkFirst will pay tuition and some other costs, even if the student does not participate in their vocational training. Supported Education coordinators can help eligible students complete WorkFirst paperwork, meet with WorkFirst staff, explain the role of Supported Education and advocate for students' choices.

APPENDICES

APPENDIX A

SUPPORTED EDUCATION SUMMARY HANDOUT

Description

Supported Education can be described as education in integrated settings for people with psychiatric disabilities for whom post-secondary education has been interrupted or intermittent as a result of a severe psychiatric disability, and who, because of their handicap, need ongoing support services to be successful in the education environment (Unger, 1990, p. 10).

Supported Education makes available curricula and training to prepare students for entry/re-entry into secondary education classrooms. The program assists each individual participant in determining education goals, as well as developing the needed accommodations and supports for success.

Mission

The mission of Supported Education is to support, assist and improve educational access and success to persons with psychiatric disabilities in the continuation of their education and recovery.

Coordination

The Supported Education Coordinator's job is to coordinate, promote, develop and implement supported education for clients of mental health services within the RSN. Responsibilities include, but are not limited to:

- Providing educational assessment and counseling to applicants, using an individualized and tailored approach;
- Facilitating or assist in teaching classes;
- Serving as an advocate for students; act as a liaison between students, the college, and other support systems to problem solve education issues;
- Informing and guiding students into college course work;
- Providing support to students in class;
- Informing and referring students to tutoring services, as they are available;
- Developing and/or adapting curricula for the Supported Education program and individual student needs;

Content

Orientation to Campus Course

Overview of resources and processes on the college campus (e.g. financial aid, admissions).

Study Skills for College Success Course

Prepares the student and upgrades skills for classroom success. Includes time management, introduction to ADA and accommodations, organizational skills, test taking preparation, classroom preparation and more.

Goal Setting/Career Planning Course

An educational and work plan is developed in this class. An interest inventory is administered, strengths and weaknesses are identified, DVR functions are clarified and goals and action steps written.

Educational Support Group

Group meets at least weekly to discuss issues and problems applicable to continuing their secondary education. Symptom management is discussed on a regular basis; natural supports are developed in the process.

Goals of Supported Education for Students/ Consumers

- Development of education and career goals;
- Improved access to public secondary education;
- Development of new skills and knowledge;
- Increase of self-confidence, and self-care;
- Assistive to the recovery process (self knowledge, hope and new life goals);

- Opportunity to prepare for GED, and complete Adult Basic Education (ABE) and High School Competition (HSC) classes, and college level course work;

- Development of natural supports and increased role in the community.

Outcomes / Trends

In Washington State, over a two-year period:

- About 50% of Supported Education students per year dropped the first time around from programs before completing the college preparation classes;

- Approximately 25% of students per year dropped to go to work or remained in college courses without further Supported Education or Supported Employment;

- An average of 25% of students who dropped, later returned to Supported Education;

- We have also seen about 10% of students re-take the same Supported Education college preparatory courses;

- One part-time coordinator has been able to serve up to approximately 30 students per quarter when the program was held at one central site, without any other staff assistance;

- From Supported Education, an average of 13% of students have taken adult basic education courses, 13% of Supported Education students took GED courses, 67% took college level courses and 10% took specific vocational training courses-17% per year graduated with a 2 or 4 year college degree or vocational training certificate;

- The average rate of student satisfaction with Supported Education programs in Washington has been 95%.

In other SEd programs, according to Weisburd (1997):

- Studies at Thresholds in Chicago and the University of Arizona have reported 47% and 41% of former Supported Education students working after participation in Supported Education;

- The University of Arizona study reported 54% of students who were in or completed Supported Education in a 6-year period were enrolled in college level courses;

- The only difference found in the resources needed to provide accommodations for students with psychiatric disabilities and people with other disabilities was greater need for more personal support by many with psychiatric disabilities (University of Arizona);

- These and other studies report that students with psychiatric disabilities tend to have higher grade point averages than other students, the retention rates tend to be about the same as other students and demographics are reported to be comparable, with the exception of age ñ average age 40 years for students with psychiatric disabilities returning to college compared to 33-34 years of age for others returning to college;

- Some indication has been found that students who enter Supported Education tend to have higher education backgrounds and more recent employment histories, diagnosis seem to be spread evenly in Supported Education programs and Supported Education students historically to have higher rates of hospitalization and issues with medications, compared to community support participants.

APPENDIX B

STORIES OF SUPPORTED EDUCATION IN LONG-TERM HOSPITALIZATIONS

Steven's Story

Steven had been hospitalized for the past four years with severe symptoms of obsessive-compulsive disorder. Prior to this time, he'd had numerous other hospitalizations. Steven was always a bright student who did well in school. His intelligence tests administered during his high school years placed him in the top 5% of his graduating class. While he was accepted to several colleges, the symptoms of his mental illness had long since developed and were worsening. He found it impossible to converse with anyone without asking repeated questions about what the intended meaning was—all part of his symptoms. He desperately wanted to take steps toward school and an eventual vocation.

Steven enrolled in computer classes at the hospital, but found that he was too advanced for the class by comparison to the other students, as well as his teacher. His symptoms made it harder and harder for him to interact without others becoming antagonized by his behavior. Few staff people would engage in conversation with him. He wrote several complaints about his computer instructor's lack of attention to his learning needs, yet he continued to pursue his education. He eventually was introduced to the Supported

Education Coordinator for possible help with enrollment in SEd courses.

He was interested in the SEd Program, but did not want to take the preparation classes, saying that he felt "beyond" these. When he met the SEd Coordinator he learned that she too was a mental health consumer. He was surprised by this news. When he began bombarding her with questions about the meaning of each thing she said, she reminded him that as a consumer, she struggled with symptoms too. This appeared to make a huge impact. He is now enrolled in the SEd preparation courses and is managing his symptoms in public settings. He is moving from the hospital setting for the first time in years. He says he likes his classes and will soon be enrolling in college level computer classes.

The Story of Lisa

Lisa was an average student in high school when she began developing problems with her family relationships and foun school increasingly hard to keep focused on. She also began using street drugs at this time. Her grades in school suffered, yet she increased her drug abuse. Finally, she quit high school and spent the next 10 years in and out of jail and rehabilitation programs for both alcohol and substance abuse treatment. Eventually, one of her counselors suggested that she be assessed for a possible mental illness. In addition to her substance abuse diagnosis, she was diagnosed with bipolar disorder.

Lisa's condition greatly worsened and she attempted suicide two times. She was hospitalized frequently and then, for a period of three years in a state psychiatric hospital. In the hospital, she learned about substance abuse and the dangers of street drugs, especially with a psychiatric disorder. She took a class at the hospital about her psychiatric disorder and became more aware of her disorder, symptoms and how to cope with those symptoms. She decided that she wanted to finish her high school diploma.

Lisa wondered if other students would notice any of her symptoms. She questioned her ability to learn again. It was at this time that a mental health technician at the hospital told her about the local Supported Education Program.

She contacted the SEd Coordinator and signed up for the first preparation course. In the educational support group, she developed several new friendships and received a lot of encouragement to continue with classes towards her high school completion. She entered college courses. She is still struggling with her ability to stay focused in the classroom, but is getting Bs and Cs. She took a three-month time out last year, but returned to the SEd Program's Student Support Group and college courses with renewed commitment. She is now talking about what Bachelor's level courses she will need to take to reach her goal of becoming a substance abuse counselor after she receives her AA diploma.

APPENDIX C

SUPPORTED EDUCATION SAMPLE SYLLABI

Sample Syllabus For Orientation to Campus

Non-Credit

- Instructor:
- Location:
- Dates:
- Time:
- Texts: All materials used for this class are resources developed and available at individual college campuses.

Course Description

This class will review a variety of typical campus resources and regulations and will assist the student in accessing and benefitting from these resources when needed. The student will develop an understanding of campus expectations and how to manage and/or reduce the incidence of stigma that potentially occurs in a campus setting.

Learning Objectives/Outcomes

The student will:

- Complete a college financial aid form and will meet with a financial aid advisor to review this information;
- Review and complete an admissions packet with an advisor;
- Demonstrate an understanding of the college code of conduct and reflect and verbalize an understanding of the Student Handbook;
- Develop a list of steps for making a student complaint;
- Develop a plan of support and a plan for managing stigma in a college environment;
- Demonstrate an understanding of college resources including testing center, library services, tutoring, etc.

Course Requirements

- Student will complete all assigned projects;
- Student will attend classes a minimum of 85% of the time

Sample Syllabus
Study Skills for College Success Course

Non-Credit

- Instructor:
- Location:
- Dates:
- Time:

Texts: Smith, Thadeus (1998). *How to be a Student.* New York, NY: Strick and James Publishers, Inc.

Course Description

This class will teach the student suceessful study methods compatible with managing a mental illness. The student will identify his/her learning style, study strategies, test-taking techniques and overall habits of a successful student. Participants will also study the role and value of the Americans with Disabilities Act (ADA) for persons with a psychiatric illness and accommodations in the process of their continuing education.

Learning Objectives

The student will:

- Learn and demonstrate recommended study methods of studying and reading materials;
- Develop and demonstrate study skills consistent with remaining healthy and stable;
- Understand the relationship between motivation and success and will develop an individualized list of ways to sustain personal motivation;
- Demonstrate successful notetaking and test-taking skills;
- Complete a written daily schedule including study times reflecting time management awareness;
- Identify at least 3 memory aids;
- Explore appropriate accommodations according to the ADA

and will identify accommodations most assistive to him/herself;

- Complete a strengths inventory and will identify personal strengths valuable to the continuing education and recovery process.

Course Requirements

The student will:

- Attend Study Skills classes a minimum of 85% of the time;
- Complete all assigned reading;
- Complete all assignments;
- Complete a final project successfully, regarding best and most useful individual accommodations.

Sample Syllabus for Goal-Setting

Non-Credit
- Instructor:
- Location:
- Dates:
- Time:
- Texts: Jones, P. J. (2001). *Educational Planning*. Fairfield, NJ: Successful Schools, Inc.

Course Description

Students in this class will investigate varied educational and vocational goals and will evaluate personal abilities, strengths, and interests. Participants will develop effective decision-making strategies and plan both short-term and long-term goals while managing the symptoms of mental illness.

Learning Objectives/Outcomes

The student will:

- Self-evaluate personal strengths, abilities, talents and special needs;
- Identify a minimum of 3 possible vocational interests;
- Demonstrate knowledge of decision-making and problem-solving strategies;
- Identify resources both professional and personal who will support efforts to meet goals;
- Develop at least 2 short-term and 2 long-term goals and a specific plan for attaining both;
- Identify likely stressors that may effect goals and a develop a plan for managing these stressors;

Course Requirements

- Student will complete a final project consisting of a plan for achieving goals;
- Student will complete all required reading;
- Student will conduct at least one informational interview;
- Student will attend class at least 85% of the time.

BIBLIOGRAPHY

Anthony, W. A. (1979). *The Principles of Psychiatric Rehabilitation*. Baltimore, MD: University Park Press.

Armstrong, William H. (1975). *Study Tips*. Woodbury, NY: Barron's Educational Series, Inc.

Department of Education (2000). PELL grants, Direct and FFEL Stafford loans, *Federal Financial Aid*. www.ed.gov/prog_info/ SFA/ StudentGuide/2000-1

Draves, William A. (1984). *How to Teach Adults*. Manhattan, KA: The Learning Resources Network (LERN).

Federal Register: February 28, 2000, The state vocational rehabilitation services program, (Volume 65, Number 39)], [Proposed Rules], [Page 10619-10665] From the Federal Register Online via GPO Access [wais.access.gpo.gov] [DOCID:fr28fe00-28] [[Page 10619]], Part III, Department of Education, 34 CFR Part 361, The State Vocational Rehabilitation Services Program; Proposed Rule, RIN 1820-AB50 Pages 10619-1062.

Frado, Lana (1993). *Learning Diversity, Accommodations in Colleges and Universities for Students with Mental Illness*. Canadian Mental Health Assoc.

Fry, Ron (1994). *How to Study.* (Third Ed.) Hawthorne, NJ: The Career Press.

Network News, Washington Department of Social and Health Services, Mental Health Division, Winter 1996.

Olivier, Carolyn and Bowler, Rosemary (1996). *Learning to Learn.* New York, NY: Simon and Schuster.

Penney, D. Redefining medical necessity: Toward development of a recovery-oriented mental health benefit, In C. Stoud, *The Complete Guide to Managed Behavioral Healthcare*. New York: John Wiley and Sons.

Roberts, M. Susan and Jansen, Gerard J. (1997). *Living With ADD: A Workbook for Adults with Attention Deficit Disorder.* Oakland, CA: New Harbinger Publications.

Semones, James K. (1991). *Effective Study Skills*. Orlando FL: Harcourt Brace College Publishers.

Smith, Sally (1991). *Succeeding Against the Odds: How the Learning Disabled Can Realize Their Promise*. New York, NY: G.P. Putnam's Sons.

State of Washington (2000). WorkSource. Http://www.wa.gov/esd/work/wsfactsheet.htm

Unger, K., (1998). *Handbook on Supported Education*. Baltimore, Maryland. Brookes Publishing Co.

Unger, Karen. Supported Education for People with Psychiatric Disabilities: Issues and Implications, in *OSERS News in Print*. Summer, 1991, American Council on Education: Health Resource Center, p. 3.

Weisburd, Dan E. (1997). Supported education, Publishers note, *The Journal of the California Alliance for the Mentally Ill.* Volume 8, Issue 2.

AUTHORS' BIOGRAPHICAL SKETCHES

Jolyn Wells-Moran, Ph.D., M.S.W., has written numerous college curricula and agency training materials, a book entitled, *Supporting People with Psychiatric Disabilities in Mental Health Employment,* and has another book, *Speaking for Myself: Self-Advocacy for People with Psychiatric Disabilities*, in process. She has been employed in the mental health field for over 20 years, managed and taught in the Consumer-To-Provider Training Program over the course of nine years, and two years ago, began the Center for Psychiatric Recovery and Rehabilitation Education (CPRRE) in Washington where she is now the Executive Director. CPRRE includes the Consumer-To-Provider Training Programs East and West and other education and training programs and services. Wells-Moran has a history of recurrent depression and speaks in various venues concerning psychiatric recovery and rehabilitation

Deanne Gilmur, M.Ed., developed the Patient and Family Education Program at Western State Hospital in Lakewood, Washington, the largest psychiatric facility in the state of Washington, and has served as Director of the program for over 20 years. She has written patient education materials for the Eli Lilly Company's series, *Team Care Solutions*, and most recently has written materials and articles for persons with psychiatric disabilities, including an article for the Journal of the California Alliance for the Mentally Ill. Deanne is a faculty member at the Washington Institute for Mental Health Education, Research and Training teaching, *Foundations of Case Management,* and in the Psychiatric Rehabilitation Certificate Program at CPRRE. She also works with colleague, Wells-Moran, to initiate and assist development of Supported Education programs through the Partnership for Development of Supported Education at CPRRE.